Container & Raised Bed Gardening for Beginners

The Ultimate Guide to Start and Design
your Homestead Garden
for all American territories.

Cultivate Your Own Vegetables, Fruits,
Medicinal Herbs, Flowers, and Plants with
Low-Budget and Simple Methods

Tommy Bloomfield

Copyright © 2024. All rights

The contents of this book may not be reproduced, duplicated, or transmitted without the written permission of the author or publisher. Under no circumstances shall the publisher, or the author, be held liable or legally responsible for any damages, compensation, or monetary loss due to the information contained in this book. Either directly or indirectly.

Legal notice: This book is copyrighted. This book is for personal use only. You may not modify, distribute, sell, use, quote, or paraphrase any part or content of this book without the consent of the author or publisher.

Introduction - Designing Your Green Haven	5
The Benefits of Growing Your Own Food	8
Embarking on a Journey of Growth and Discovery	11
Chapter 1: Designing Your Green Haven	14
Assessing Available Space and Sunlight	14
Choosing the Right Structures for Your Needs	17
Designing Your Garden Layout to Optimize Space	20
Chapter 2: The Foundation of Growth: Building Your Garden Beds	23
Materials Needed and Where to Find Them	23
Step-by-Step Instructions for Construction	26
Tips for Low-Cost Construction	29
Chapter 3: Mastering Container Gardening	33
Container Selection	33
The Importance of Drainage	36
Benefits of Container Gardening	39
Chapter 4: Plant Selection & Maintenance	43
A Care Guide for Common Plants	46
Planting and Harvesting Calendar: The Gardener's Almanac	49
Chapter 5: Soil Science: Creating a Fertile Foundation	54
Creating and maintaining fertile soil	54
Composting and Natural Fertilizers: The Lifeblood of the Garden	57
Soil testing and pH adjustment	59
Chapter 6: The Art of Watering: Irrigation Strategies	63
Do-it-yourself irrigation systems	63

    Frequency and quantity of watering   66

    Water conservation and rainwater harvesting   68

Chapter 7: Managing Pests and Diseases   72

    Ecological identification and treatment   72

    Prevention through garden design   74

    Natural and safe remedies   77

Chapter 8: The Harvest Cycle: From Garden to Table   81

    Harvesting Techniques to Maximize Yield   81

    Storage and use of vegetables   84

    Simple recipes for enjoying your harvest   86

Chapter 9: Gardening Through the Seasons: Year-Round Care   89

    Calendar of gardening tasks   89

    Preparing for the change of seasons   93

    Renovating and restoring the garden   95

    Conclusion   98

Chapter 10: Troubleshooting in the Garden: Solutions and Tips   99

    Diagnosing and Solving Frequent Problems in the Garden   99

    When and How to Ask for Help in the Garden   102

    Maintaining Motivation Amidst the Verdant Labyrinth   104

Conclusion   107

BONUS   110

Introduction - Designing Your Green Haven

Embarking on the journey to create your personal green haven is not just about planting seeds and watching them grow; it's about cultivating a relationship with nature, right at your doorstep. This endeavor is both an art and a science, a venture where patience meets creativity, leading to the birth of a living tapestry that thrives under your care. It's about transforming a mere patch of land or a collection of containers into a vibrant sanctuary that nourishes both the body and soul. As we delve into the process of designing your garden, we embark on a quest to create a space that reflects your personal aesthetics, caters to your nutritional needs, and harmonizes with the environment.

The initial step in this journey is visualizing the space. Picture your garden not just as a place of cultivation but as a sanctuary where you can reconnect with nature, find peace, and experience the joy of nurturing life. Whether you have a sprawling backyard or a modest balcony, every space holds the potential to become a verdant retreat. Imagine stepping into your garden and being greeted by a kaleidoscope of colors, the subtle fragrance of herbs and flowers, and the tranquil sound of bees busily pollinating. This vision will guide your decisions, from the selection of plants to the layout of your garden beds and containers.

In designing your green haven, consider the interplay of light and shadow throughout the day. Sunlight is the lifeblood of your garden, dictating which plants will thrive in certain areas. Observe how the sun bathes your space at different times, and use this knowledge to create a living painting that changes hues with the passing hours. The dance of light and shadow will not only influence the health of your plants but also create a dynamic landscape that captures the beauty of the natural world.

Choosing the right structures for your garden is akin to selecting the frame for a masterpiece. Raised beds and containers offer a versatile canvas for your horticultural creations. They allow for better soil control, ease of maintenance, and can be designed to fit any aesthetic. Raised beds, with their elevated stature, bring the garden closer to you, making it easier to tend to your plants without straining your back. Containers, on the other hand, are the epitome of flexibility, enabling you to grow plants in spaces where traditional gardens would be impractical. They can be moved to capture the best light, rotated to encourage even growth, and arranged to create a living mosaic that enhances your living space.

The design of your garden layout is not merely about aesthetics; it's a thoughtful process that optimizes space and promotes the health of your plants. Consider the companionship between different plant species; some thrive together, sharing nutrients and deterring pests, while others may compete for resources. By understanding these relationships, you can create a garden that is not only beautiful but also a self-sustaining ecosystem. The layout should also consider ease of access for maintenance and harvesting, ensuring that every plant can be easily reached and cared for.

Incorporating elements of sustainable gardening practices from the start sets the foundation for a garden that is in harmony with the environment. Collecting rainwater, creating compost from kitchen scraps, and selecting native plants are just a few ways to reduce your environmental footprint and create a garden that thrives with minimal intervention. These practices not only benefit the planet but also enrich your garden, creating a cycle of nourishment that supports both the land and your well-being.

As you design your green haven, remember that gardening is a journey of discovery and learning. Each plant has its unique needs and gifts, and part of the joy is getting to know them, understanding their language, and watching them flourish under your care. Your garden will evolve with each season, each year becoming more intertwined with your life, reflecting your growth and changes. It becomes a living diary, chronicling your connection with the earth and the cycles of life. Designing your garden is also an opportunity to express your creativity and personal style. From the rustic charm of wooden raised beds to the sleek elegance of ceramic containers, your garden is a reflection of your aesthetic. The colors, textures, and scents of the plants you choose create a sensory experience that is uniquely yours. Your garden can be a place of serene beauty, a vibrant playground of colors, or a practical source of herbs and vegetables. The possibilities are as limitless as your imagination.

In the end, your green haven is more than just a garden; it's a sanctuary where life is nurtured, a place of learning and growth, and a canvas for creative expression. It's a testament to the resilience of life and the beauty of nature. As you embark on this journey, remember that every choice you make, from the layout of your garden to the plants you nurture, contributes to the creation of a space that not only grows plants but also cultivates happiness, health, and a deeper connection with the natural world.

The Benefits of Growing Your Own Food

In the heart of every seed lies the dormant promise of a plant waiting to stretch towards the sun, a symbol of life's resilience and the foundation of our sustenance. The act of nurturing these seeds into flourishing plants is not just an ancient practice passed down through generations but a transformative experience that reconnects us to the earth and to the very essence of life. Growing your own food is an act of creation, a journey that is as nourishing to the soul as it is to the body.

The benefits of cultivating your own garden are manifold, transcending the simple act of planting and harvesting. It is a pathway to wellness, where the rhythm of nature guides the ebb and flow of life. The garden becomes a sanctuary, a place of tranquility and reflection, where the worries of the world dissipate in the soil, leaving behind a sense of peace and a connection to something greater than ourselves. This connection to the earth, to the cycles of growth and decay, reminds us of our place in the natural world, fostering a sense of stewardship and respect for the environment that sustains us.

Nutritional richness is another cornerstone of growing your own food. Vegetables and fruits harvested fresh from the garden are at their peak of nutritional value, laden with vitamins, minerals, and antioxidants that are essential for robust health. The difference in taste and quality is incomparable, with flavors that are as vibrant as the colors of the produce. This bounty not only nourishes the body but also inspires a palette of culinary creativity, transforming meals into a celebration of the seasons and the fruits of your labor.

Sustainability is a key benefit of home gardening, offering a practical solution to the environmental challenges of our time. By cultivating your own food, you reduce your carbon footprint, minimize the need for plastic packaging, and contribute to the preservation of precious resources like water and soil. Composting kitchen scraps and garden waste closes the loop, creating a cycle of regeneration that enriches the soil and promotes biodiversity. This sustainable practice is a step towards healing the planet, one garden at a time.

Economic savings are not to be overlooked in the equation of home gardening. The initial investment in seeds, soil, and perhaps some basic tools is offset by the abundance of produce that can be harvested throughout the season. The cost savings are significant when compared to purchasing organic produce from the store, not to mention the immeasurable value of the joy and satisfaction derived from growing your own food. It is an investment in your health, your well-being, and the environment, yielding dividends that extend far beyond the garden.

The educational opportunities presented by gardening are boundless, offering lessons in patience, responsibility, and the intricacies of life cycles. For children, a garden is a classroom without walls, a place of discovery and wonder that ignites curiosity and fosters a sense of responsibility towards the natural world. For adults, it is a reminder of the marvels of nature, an opportunity to learn new skills, and a challenge to adapt and grow. Gardening is a lifelong journey of learning, where every season brings new insights and surprises.

Community and connection are cultivated in the garden, where the sharing of seeds, produce, and knowledge strengthens bonds and builds networks of support. Gardens become the common ground where differences fade away, replaced by the shared experience of growth and the universal language of nature. This sense of community extends beyond the physical boundaries of the garden, creating ripples that enrich the social fabric of neighborhoods and beyond.

In conclusion, the benefits of growing your own food are as diverse as the gardens that dot our landscapes. They weave together threads of wellness, sustainability, economy, education, community, and connection into a tapestry that reflects the beauty and complexity of life. The garden is a mirror of the soul, a place where we can learn, grow, and connect with the essence of who we are and the world we inhabit. It is a journey back to the roots, to the simple yet profound act of nurturing life, and in doing so, nurturing ourselves.

Embarking on a Journey of Growth and Discovery

As you hold this book in your hands, poised at the threshold of a journey both literal and metaphorical, you embark on a quest not just of gardening but of transformation. This guide, your companion in the endeavor, is designed not merely to instruct but to inspire, leading you through the nuanced tapestry of raised bed and container gardening with wisdom, empathy, and understanding. Within these pages lies more than knowledge; here, we weave a narrative of connection—a dialogue between you and the earth, between seed and soil. This book is an invitation to engage in a dance as ancient as time, yet as fresh as the morning dew, a call to arms in the gentlest sense, where the tools of our trade are trowels and seeds, and our battlegrounds are the beds and containers that will cradle life.

This journey is one of discovery, where each chapter unfolds like the petals of a bloom, revealing layer upon layer of insights and revelations. Here, we delve into the heart of gardening, exploring the alchemy of soil and seed, the rhythm of seasons, and the joy of harvest. This is a guide that transcends the mechanical act of planting and watering, elevating gardening to a sacred act of creation, a testament to the resilience of life.

As your guide, this book does not walk a straight, narrow path but meanders, following the whimsy of nature itself, exploring the tangents where beauty and utility intersect. We explore the art and science of gardening, from the tactile pleasure of soil between your fingers to the precise calculations that ensure the health and vitality of your garden. This is a holistic approach, recognizing that gardening is not just about the end product but about the process—the moments of quiet contemplation, the bursts of intense activity, and the inevitable setbacks and triumphs.

In these pages, you will not find simple prescriptions or one-size-fits-all solutions. Instead, we offer principles and practices that honor the uniqueness of each garden and gardener. We acknowledge that each plot of soil, each container, holds its own potential and challenges, just as each gardener brings their own dreams and limitations to the table. This book is a map, but you are the explorer, charting your own course through the world of gardening.

We address the practicalities of gardening, from selecting the right tools and materials to understanding the nuances of light, water, and nutrients. Yet, we also delve deeper, inviting you to ponder the ethics of gardening, the environmental impact of your choices, and the ways in which your garden can become a sanctuary for you and for the wildlife that shares our world.

This guide is rich with stories—not just our own, but those of countless gardeners who have walked this path before you. These anecdotes serve not just to enlighten but to connect, reminding us that gardening is a shared human experience, transcending time and culture. Through these stories, we offer not just instruction but solace, inspiration, and companionship. As you progress through the chapters, you'll find that gardening is more than a hobby; it's a way of life. It's a practice that cultivates patience, resilience, and a deep appreciation for the simple things that sustain us. This book is your invitation to slow down, to connect with the earth, and to find joy in the growth and flourishing of life under your care. This journey you're about to embark upon is one of endless learning and discovery. Each season, each harvest, brings new lessons, new challenges, and new rewards. This book is a testament to the cycles of life, a guide that will grow with you as you evolve from a novice gardener into a steward of the earth. It's a reminder that, in gardening, as in life, the journey is the destination.

As you turn these pages, know that you're not just learning to garden; you're gardening to learn. About the earth, about yourself, and about the intricate web of life that connects us all. Welcome to your green haven, a place of growth, renewal, and connection. Welcome to the journey.

Chapter 1: Designing Your Green Haven

Assessing Available Space and Sunlight

Embarking on the journey of creating your green haven begins with a seemingly simple yet profoundly critical step: evaluating the space and sunlight available to you. This foundational assessment shapes the entire trajectory of your garden, influencing not just what you can grow but how your garden integrates with your life and home.

Imagine standing at the threshold of your potential garden space. It might be a compact balcony in a bustling city, a sprawling backyard in the suburbs, or even a modest patch of land by your townhouse. The size and location of this space are your canvas; understanding its dimensions and characteristics is akin to a painter understanding their palette before the brush even hits the canvas.

The first dimension to consider is the physical space. Measure the length and width of your potential gardening area. These measurements are not just numbers; they represent the potential for life, growth, and sustenance. As you jot these down, consider the vertical space as well. Urban gardeners, in particular, find that looking up opens a new realm of possibilities. Trellises, hanging baskets, and wall-mounted planters can transform a bare balcony or a small patio into a lush, tiered garden.

Now, turn your attention to the sun, the lifeblood of your garden. The amount of sunlight your space receives is not a mere detail; it is a guiding light for your gardening endeavors. Monitor the sunlight over a few days, noting the hours of direct sunlight versus partial shade. This natural illumination dictates the plants that will thrive in your space. A south-facing garden basks in sunlight for most of the day, welcoming a wide array of sun-loving plants. Conversely, a north-facing area, swathed in gentle shade, calls for plants that flourish under a softer glow.

Understanding your space's sun exposure also involves recognizing the sun's journey across the sky throughout the year. The angle and intensity of sunlight change with the seasons, affecting how plants grow. A spot that basks in full sun during the summer months might receive significantly less light in the winter, influencing not just what you can grow but when.

As you consider the space and sunlight available to you, remember that constraints can foster creativity. A limited area challenges you to think innovatively about using vertical space and choosing plants that grow well together. Limited sunlight encourages you to explore the rich diversity of shade-tolerant plants, many of which offer lush foliage and vibrant flowers.

The relationship between your space and the sun is a delicate dance. Some areas of your garden might see a kaleidoscope of light patterns throughout the day, a patchwork of sun and shade as the sun moves across the sky. These nuances are not obstacles but opportunities to create a dynamic garden that changes mood and character with the passing hours.

In assessing your space, consider also the microclimates within your garden. Areas sheltered by walls or fences might retain heat, creating warm pockets ideal for plants that crave warmth. Conversely, open areas might be cooler or more prone to winds, guiding you towards hardier, resilient plant choices.

Your garden's orientation relative to the sun and its microclimates are not static; they interact with the changing seasons, the weather, and even the growth of the plants themselves. As trees and shrubs mature, they cast new shadows, creating cooler areas beneath their canopy. This evolving landscape invites you to be flexible, to observe and adapt, embracing the garden's dynamic nature.

As you embark on this journey, remember that your green haven is not just about the plants you grow but the ecosystem you create. Assessing your space and sunlight is the first step in a dialogue with nature, a conversation that will guide every decision in your garden. This initial assessment lays the foundation for a garden that is not only beautiful but also resilient, sustainable, and harmoniously integrated with its environment. In embracing this first step, you're not just planning a garden; you're crafting a sanctuary. A place where nature's rhythms guide your hand, where each plant chosen is a reflection of the light and space it calls home. Your green haven is a testament to the beauty that arises when we listen to and work with the natural world around us.

This journey of assessment is just the beginning, a first step in creating a space that reflects your unique vision and the possibilities inherent in your slice of the natural world. As you move forward, let the knowledge of your space and sunlight be your guide, illuminating the path to a garden that is not only a source of beauty and sustenance but a haven for the soul.

Choosing the Right Structures for Your Needs

Selecting the appropriate structures for your garden transcends mere aesthetics or practicality. It is about weaving your dreams into the fabric of reality, about creating a space that resonates with your soul and meets the needs of the plants you wish to nurture. This choice is a confluence of vision and functionality, a decision that will shape the essence of your green haven.

Imagine your garden as a blank canvas, and the structures you choose as the strokes of paint that bring it to life. Whether it's raised beds, containers, trellises, or greenhouses, each structure has its own story, its own way of interacting with the light, the wind, and the soil. Your task is to select the ones that best complement your space, your climate, and your gardening aspirations.

Raised beds, for instance, are not just wooden boxes filled with soil. They are elevated sanctuaries that offer your plants protection from soil compaction, improved drainage, and a warmer growing medium. They are particularly beneficial for gardeners dealing with challenging soil conditions or those who seek to maximize their yields in a limited space. The choice of materials for these beds—whether cedar, redwood, or recycled composite—adds another layer to your garden's narrative, reflecting your commitment to sustainability or durability.

Containers, on the other hand, are the nomads of the garden world. They offer unparalleled flexibility, allowing you to create a movable feast of color and life. From terracotta pots that whisper tales of the earth to modern resin containers that speak of innovation and resilience, the variety is endless. Containers are the answer for those who wish to chase the sun, moving their plants to capture the light or shelter them from the elements. They are ideal for cultivating everything from a simple herb garden to a lush array of flowering annuals and perennials.

Trellises and support structures introduce verticality to your garden, transforming it from a flat tapestry to a three-dimensional living sculpture. They invite you to look up, to dream bigger. Vines clinging to a trellis, beans spiraling up a pole, or tomatoes supported by sturdy cages add height and depth, creating layers of greenery that enchant the eye and maximize your growing space. These structures are not just supports; they are the backbone of your garden, enabling it to reach upwards towards the sky.

The greenhouse, whether a sprawling structure or a modest cold frame, is a testament to the gardener's ambition to defy the seasons. It is a microcosm of the garden's potential, a place where warmth and humidity nurture seedlings into vibrant life, offering a head start in colder climates or a year-round sanctuary for tender plants. The greenhouse is a commitment to gardening as a way of life, a space where the green thumb is not limited by the whims of weather.

Selecting the right structures for your garden is an act of balance. It requires an understanding of your garden's unique characteristics—the quality of sunlight, the patterns of wind and rain, and the temperament of your soil. It also demands an introspection into your own desires. Do you seek the simplicity and elegance of a minimalist garden, or do you revel in the abundance and variety of a cottage garden? Your structures should reflect not only the practical needs of your plants but also the aesthetic and emotional aspirations of your heart.

In making these choices, consider the longevity and maintenance of the structures you introduce into your garden. A raised bed may require replenishment of soil or repair of its frame, while containers might need regular replacement or repainting. Trellises and supports may need to be sturdy enough to withstand the weight of mature plants and the fury of storms. These considerations are integral to creating a garden that is not just beautiful today but sustainable for many seasons to come.

The structures you choose are the bones of your garden, the framework upon which the flesh of leaves, flowers, and fruits will grow. They are a reflection of your commitment to creating a space that is not only productive but also personal and profound. As you select these structures, let them be a reflection of your journey as a gardener—a journey that is about more than just plants. It is about creating a sanctuary for yourself, a green haven where the soul can flourish alongside the garden.

In choosing the right structures for your needs, you are not just planning a garden; you are sculpting a living, breathing piece of art. This art is not static; it grows and changes with each passing season, shaped by your hands and nurtured by your care. It is a testament to the power of growth, the beauty of nature, and the endless possibilities that lie in a patch of earth and a seed of dream.

Designing Your Garden Layout to Optimize Space

Crafting the layout of your garden is akin to composing a symphony. Each element, from the smallest herb to the tallest sunflower, plays its part in the harmony of your green space. This task, while daunting at first glance, unfolds as a journey of creativity and strategic thinking, guiding you to make the most of every inch of your garden.

Imagine your garden space as a blank canvas, yet one that whispers the potential of lush greenery and vibrant blooms. The design of this canvas is not merely about placing plants where there's room; it's about envisioning the interplay of light and shadow, the dance of colors and textures, and the rhythm of growth through the seasons. Your goal is to create a living mosaic that delights the senses, supports the ecosystem, and yields an abundance of produce and beauty.

The heart of optimizing garden space lies in understanding the unique dimensions and potential of your area. It's about recognizing that even the smallest patch of earth can host a diversity of life, provided it's planned with care and imagination. Start by sketching a rough map of your garden, noting areas of full sun, partial shade, and full shade. These notes become the guideposts for plant selection and placement, ensuring that each plant thrives in its designated spot, contributing to the overall well-being of the garden ecosystem.

Next, consider the vertical dimension of your space. Vertical gardening is not just a trend; it's a revelation in maximizing space and adding depth to your garden. Trellises for climbing plants, wall-mounted planters for herbs, and hanging baskets for trailing blooms are just a few ways to elevate your garden literally and figuratively. This approach allows you to grow upwards, expanding your garden's capacity without spreading outwards, making it ideal for small spaces. Integrating companion planting into your layout is another strategy for optimizing space. This age-old practice involves placing plants together that benefit each other in terms of growth, pest control, and pollination. For instance, planting basil near tomatoes not only saves space but also helps repel pests and improve flavor. Such synergies not only maximize the productivity of your garden but also enhance its health and biodiversity.

The design of your garden layout should also consider the temporal aspect of gardening—the succession of crops. Succession planting, where you plant new crops as others are harvested, ensures a continuous supply of produce. This method requires careful planning to make sure that as one plant's journey ends, another begins, keeping the soil active and your garden flourishing throughout the growing season.

In the quest to optimize space, it's essential to embrace flexibility and creativity. A garden is a living entity, constantly evolving with the seasons, the weather, and the gardener's touch. Your initial layout might change as you discover which plants flourish and which struggle, or as you adapt to the changing needs of your garden and your own desires. This flexibility allows your garden to be a reflection of your learning and growth as a gardener, evolving into a space that is uniquely yours. The design of your garden should also be a sanctuary for you, the gardener. Paths that invite you to wander, spaces for sitting and reflecting, and areas designed for interaction with the plants make the garden not just a place of production but a haven of peace and connection with nature. These elements of design remind us that gardens are not just about the end product but about the process—the joy of tending, growing, and being in harmony with the natural world.

Creating a garden layout that optimizes space is not just about efficient use of physical dimensions; it's about crafting a space that nourishes the body, soothes the soul, and brings life to the community. It's a testament to the fact that with thoughtful planning and a creative spirit, even the smallest garden can be a bastion of abundance, beauty, and sustainability.

As you design your garden layout, remember that each decision you make—from the placement of a trellis to the choice of companion plants—is a stroke in the larger painting of your garden. This process, rich with potential and discovery, is your journey to creating a green haven that reflects your vision, your care, and your love for the earth. It's a reminder that in the world of gardening, limitations are but invitations to innovate, to dream, and to create spaces that resonate with life and possibility.

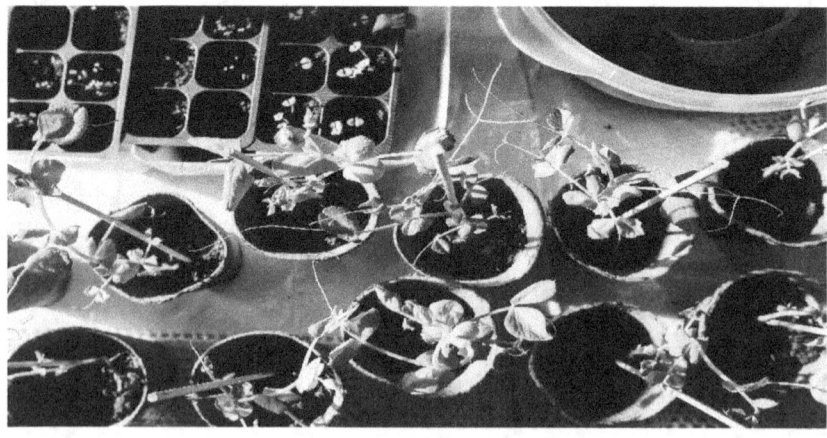

Chapter 2: The Foundation of Growth: Building Your Garden Beds

Materials Needed and Where to Find Them

Embarking on the journey of building your garden beds is akin to setting the stage for a grand performance. The materials you choose and where you source them from are pivotal decisions that lay the groundwork for a thriving garden. This foundation is not merely about soil and seeds; it's about creating an environment where life can flourish, where your efforts as a gardener are rewarded with growth, beauty, and bounty.

The selection of materials for your garden beds is a reflection of your values and aspirations. It's about harmonizing with nature, ensuring sustainability, and nurturing life from the ground up. Each material has its story, its essence, and its impact on the earth and your garden.

Wood is a popular choice for raised beds, offering natural beauty, durability, and breathability. Cedar and redwood are prized for their resistance to rot and pests, embodying the resilience and strength of nature. These woods whisper tales of ancient forests and enduring landscapes, bringing a piece of the wilderness into your garden. Sourcing sustainably harvested wood or using reclaimed lumber not only reduces your environmental footprint but also adds a layer of history and character to your garden beds.

Recycled materials offer another avenue for gardeners to tread lightly on the earth. Composite decking, repurposed bricks, and even salvaged railway ties can be transformed into unique and eco-friendly garden beds. These materials speak of a commitment to sustainability, a testament to the gardener's role as a steward of the planet. Local recycling centers, construction sites, and online marketplaces are treasure troves for these gems, waiting to be rediscovered and given a new life in your garden.

For those seeking a modern twist, metal garden beds made of galvanized steel or aluminum present a sleek and sturdy alternative. These materials dance with the light, adding a contemporary edge to the garden while offering longevity and protection against pests and decay. Metal beds can be sourced from garden supply stores or custom fabricated to fit your unique vision, providing a clean and minimalist aesthetic that contrasts beautifully with the softness of greenery and soil.

Stone and concrete blocks offer a timeless elegance, grounding your garden with a sense of permanence and stability. These materials, sourced from local quarries or landscape suppliers, evoke the majesty of mountains and the tranquility of ancient gardens. Building with stone or concrete is an ode to the enduring relationship between human craftsmanship and natural beauty, creating garden beds that are as much a work of art as they are functional growing spaces.

Beyond the hard materials, the choice of soil is perhaps the most critical decision in creating your garden beds. Rich, fertile soil is the heart of the garden, the medium through which life grows. Compost, peat moss, vermiculite, and well-rotted manure are the building blocks of a healthy soil mix, each contributing to the texture, nutrition, and moisture retention of the bed.

Local garden centers, compost facilities, and farming cooperatives are invaluable resources for sourcing high-quality soil and amendments, ensuring your garden has the best possible foundation for growth.

As you gather materials for your garden beds, consider the journey they've taken to reach you. The sustainability of your garden begins with these choices, each one an opportunity to connect with local businesses, support ethical practices, and reduce your environmental impact. Flea markets, garage sales, and community networks are also excellent sources for materials, offering a chance to repurpose and recycle while building connections within your community.

In selecting materials, balance aesthetics with functionality, sustainability with cost. It's a delicate dance, one that requires thoughtfulness and care. Your garden beds are not just containers for plants; they are expressions of your relationship with the earth, manifestations of your commitment to nurturing life in harmony with nature.

Building your garden beds is an act of creation, a collaboration between you, the materials you choose, and the natural world. It's a process filled with anticipation, envisioning the future blooms and harvests that will spring from this foundation. As you lay each board, stone, or block, you're not just constructing garden beds; you're laying the groundwork for a sanctuary of growth, a space where life thrives under your care and stewardship.

In this endeavor, let your heart guide you. Choose materials that speak to you, that resonate with your vision for your garden and your hopes for the environment. Your garden beds are the first step in a journey of growth and discovery, a testament to the beauty and abundance that can be created when we work in harmony with nature. This foundation you build today is the soil from which tomorrow's dreams will grow, a legacy of life and beauty that begins with the simple act of choosing and gathering the right materials.

Step-by-Step Instructions for Construction

Embarking on the construction of your garden beds is a journey that begins with a vision and culminates in the creation of a nurturing space for your plants to flourish. This process is a dance between the gardener and the earth, a series of steps that transforms raw materials into a haven for growth.

As you stand before the space that will soon become your garden, take a moment to envision the life that will emerge from it. The beds you are about to construct will become the cradle for delicate seedlings and the stronghold for burgeoning plants. This is not just about building; it's about creating a space where life can thrive in harmony with nature.

1. Gathering Your Materials and Tools

With your materials at hand, sourced with care and consideration for sustainability and quality, lay them out with reverence. These are not merely planks of wood, screws, and soil; they are the elements from which your garden will grow. Your tools, too, are extensions of your hands, ready to transform vision into reality.

2. Measuring and Marking the Ground

Begin by measuring the ground, marking the corners of your future garden beds with stakes. Use a string to outline the perimeters, a guide for your path forward. This act of marking the ground is a declaration of intent, a first step in bringing your garden to life.

3. Cutting Your Materials to Size

With precision and care, cut your wood or other materials to the desired lengths, each piece a building block for your garden beds. This step requires patience and attention to detail, as the foundation of your garden beds must be strong and true.

4. Assembling the Frame

Lay out the cut pieces on the ground, forming the outline of your garden bed. Begin to assemble the frame, attaching the corners with screws or brackets. As you work, imagine the frame as a vessel for growth, its integrity essential for the life it will support.

5. Preparing the Site

Clear the site of your garden bed, removing weeds, stones, and debris. This preparation is an act of clearing away the old, making room for the new growth that will soon take root. Level the ground as much as possible, for a stable foundation is key to a thriving garden.

6. Positioning the Frame

With the site prepared, gently place the frame onto the ground. Adjust it so that it sits level and firmly in its designated space. This is the moment when your garden bed begins to take its place in the landscape, a tangible manifestation of your vision.

7. Adding Soil and Compost

Now, fill the frame with soil, rich and fertile. Layer in compost, the essence of life, to nourish your plants. As you shovel the soil and compost into the bed, consider this an act of giving, providing your plants with the nutrients they need to grow strong and healthy.

8. Watering the Bed

With the bed filled, water it thoroughly, allowing moisture to seep deep into the soil. This water is the first drink for your garden, a vital element that will sustain it through its growth.

9. Planting Your Seeds or Seedlings

Finally, the moment of planting arrives. Whether you are sowing seeds or transplanting seedlings, do so with a gentle hand and a hopeful heart. Each seed, each plant, is a promise of future harvests, of beauty and abundance yet to come.

10. Reflecting on Your Work

As you step back to admire your newly constructed garden bed, take a moment to reflect on the journey you've undertaken. From gathering materials to planting, each step has been a part of a larger process of creation. Your garden bed, now a reality, is a testament to your dedication, a space where life will unfold in its myriad forms.

Constructing your garden beds is more than a series of tasks; it's a journey of connection with the earth and a celebration of the cycle of life. With each bed you build, you lay the foundation for growth, not just for your plants, but for yourself as a gardener and a steward of the earth. This process, from the first measurement to the last planted seed, is a narrative of hope and growth, a story that you will continue to write with each season that passes in your green haven.

Tips for Low-Cost Construction

In the heart of every gardener beats a dream of lush, thriving gardens that don't strain the wallet. The art of constructing garden beds on a budget is akin to a dance between necessity and creativity, where resourcefulness leads the way to cultivating a flourishing haven without the burden of excessive costs. This journey of low-cost construction is not merely about saving money; it's about embracing sustainability, ingenuity, and the joy of creating something beautiful from the humblest of materials.

Embarking on this path requires a shift in perspective, seeing potential in the overlooked and value in the reclaimed. The first step is sourcing materials that are both cost-effective and durable, laying the groundwork for garden beds that will nurture life season after season. Pallets, discarded with disregard by many, are treasure troves of sturdy wood waiting to be transformed into raised beds. With a keen eye and a bit of effort, these pallets can be dismantled and repurposed, their planks reborn as the walls of your garden beds.

Local classified ads and community sharing platforms are wellsprings of materials offered at little to no cost. Here, one might find bricks longing for a second life, defining the edges of a new garden bed, or cinder blocks that, when arranged with care, become both the structure and the aesthetic of a minimalist garden space. Engaging with your community in this way not only reduces your expenses but also strengthens the bonds between neighbors, as you share resources and support each other's gardening endeavors.

Another avenue for low-cost construction is the use of natural materials gathered from your surroundings. Fallen branches, stones, and even dense clumps of earth can be fashioned into rustic, organic garden beds. These materials, offered freely by nature, require only the investment of your time and labor. Constructing beds from such materials is a testament to the gardener's harmony with the environment, each stone placed by hand, each branch woven into the fabric of the garden.

The construction process itself is an area ripe for savings. By employing simple tools and techniques, you can build your garden beds without the need for expensive equipment or professional assistance. Basic hand tools, a spirit of DIY, and the wealth of knowledge available in community workshops and online tutorials empower you to take the construction into your own hands. This approach not only saves money but also imbues your garden with a personal touch, each nail driven and each board cut a direct expression of your dedication to your garden.

Innovation in design also plays a crucial role in reducing costs. Exploring vertical gardening, for instance, maximizes your growing space without the need for extensive ground preparation or materials. Trellises made from repurposed materials can support climbing plants, turning a simple wall or fence into a verdant cascade of vegetables and flowers. This efficient use of space and resources exemplifies the creative spirit of low-cost gardening, where limitations become the mother of invention.

Water conservation techniques, such as the use of mulch derived from yard waste or the installation of simple drip irrigation systems made from recycled containers, further reduce the costs associated with maintaining your garden beds. These practices, sustainable in both environmental and financial terms, ensure that your garden thrives while conserving precious resources.

The philosophy of low-cost construction extends beyond the mere physical creation of garden beds. It encompasses a holistic approach to gardening, where every decision, from the selection of plants to the methods of pest control, is made with an eye toward sustainability and self-reliance. Choosing native plants that require less water and care, employing natural pest deterrents, and creating your own compost from kitchen and garden waste are all practices that reduce the need for purchased inputs, closing the loop of your garden's ecosystem.

Constructing your garden beds with minimal financial investment is a journey of discovery, a challenge that calls forth creativity, resourcefulness, and a deep connection to the land. It's about finding beauty in simplicity, strength in sustainability, and abundance in what the earth offers freely. As you lay each stone, turn each screw, and fill each bed with soil, remember that the value of your garden is not measured in currency, but in the life it sustains, the joy it brings, and the harmony it creates between you and the natural world.

In this endeavor, your garden becomes a canvas not only for plants but for your ingenuity and spirit. The low-cost construction of your garden beds is a testament to the idea that with creativity, passion, and a willingness to see potential where others see waste, you can create a haven that nurtures both the environment and your soul. This approach to gardening, grounded in care for the earth and mindful consumption, is a path to a greener, more sustainable future, one garden bed at a time.

Chapter 3: Mastering Container Gardening

Container Selection

The choice of container is the first and perhaps most crucial decision in the art of container gardening. It's not just about picking a pot; it's about setting the stage for a miniature ecosystem to thrive. This initial step transcends mere aesthetics, delving into the essence of what it means to create a nurturing environment for plants outside of the traditional garden bed. Selecting the right container is akin to choosing a home for your plants—a decision that influences their health, growth, and the overall harmony of your garden space.

Imagine each container as a microcosm, a small world where roots spread, stems grow, and flowers bloom. The size, material, and design of the container all play pivotal roles in this delicate ballet of life. Size dictates the root space available for your plants, directly impacting their health and growth. A pot too small stifles a plant, cramping its roots and limiting its potential, while one too large risks moisture imbalance, leading to root rot or drought stress. The key lies in finding a balance, selecting a size that allows for growth but maintains the cozy embrace plants need to feel secure and thrive.

The material of the container adds another layer to this complex decision. Clay and terracotta breathe with the earth, offering a porous home that allows air and moisture to move freely, echoing the natural rhythms of the garden. These materials, with their earthy tones and textures, bring a piece of the ancient world into your modern garden, blending tradition with the present.

However, their porous nature also demands more frequent watering, a consideration for the attentive gardener.

Plastic and resin containers, on the other hand, are the nomads of the garden world. Lightweight and versatile, they make gardens mobile, bringing greenery to patios, balconies, and beyond. These materials retain moisture longer, reducing watering needs but requiring vigilance to avoid waterlogging. Their range of colors and designs offer a palette for personal expression, turning each container into a statement of style.

Metal pots introduce an element of industrial chic, a contrast between the softness of plant life and the hardness of human craft. Yet, they conduct heat, warming soil on sunny days, and chilling it when the temperature drops. This duality demands a gardener's wisdom to place metal containers where they can bask in the sun's glory without overheating their verdant inhabitants.

Wooden containers are the bridge between the natural and the nurtured garden. They blend seamlessly with the outdoor environment, aging gracefully into silvery patinas that tell stories of seasons past. Wood insulates soil from extreme temperature changes, offering a stable environment for roots. Yet, its organic nature means it will eventually return to the earth, a cycle of life and decay that requires periodic replacement.

Beyond the physical attributes, the design of the container is a canvas for creativity. From the sleek lines of modern planters to the rustic charm of repurposed objects, the design reflects the gardener's personality and the thematic essence of the garden. A whimsically painted pot can become a focal point, a conversation starter, or a piece of living art. Similarly, a simple, elegant container can underscore the beauty of the plant it holds, allowing the greenery to be the star of the show.

In selecting containers, one must also consider the symbiosis between plant and pot. Some plants prefer tight quarters, their roots embracing the confines of their container, while others require room to roam. Understanding the nature of your plants, their needs, and desires, is essential in choosing their perfect home. This relationship between container and plant is a dialogue, a give-and-take that guides the gardener in creating a harmonious space.

The selection of containers is more than a preliminary step in container gardening; it is a foundational act of creation. It involves understanding the balance of elements—air, water, earth—and how they interact within the confines of a pot. It's about envisioning the future, imagining the plant in full bloom, its roots spread in a happy, healthy network within the chosen container. This vision guides the gardener in making selections that not only meet the practical needs of the plants but also express the aesthetic and emotional aspirations of the gardener.

Container gardening is an art form, where the pot is as much a part of the garden as the plants it holds. The selection of containers is a process imbued with intention, care, and creativity, a reflection of the gardener's connection to the earth and their commitment to nurturing life in all its forms. In this act of selection, gardeners weave together the threads of nature and nurture, crafting spaces that are as diverse, vibrant, and resilient as the world around us. This is the essence of pot culture, a celebration of life in its most compact and expressive form.

The Importance of Drainage

In the realm of container gardening, drainage is not merely a functional requirement; it's a critical lifeline for every plant thriving in the confined ecosystem of a pot. This aspect of gardening transcends the basic understanding of water flow, delving deep into the very essence of plant health, growth dynamics, and the delicate balance of moisture that spells the difference between flourishing life and untimely decay. The importance of drainage is a testament to the gardener's understanding and respect for the natural requirements of plants, showcasing a commitment to creating environments where nature's artistry can be displayed in its full glory. Drainage is the unsung hero of container gardening, a guardian against the perils of overwatering and waterlogged roots. It stands as a critical checkpoint in the journey of water from the moment it kisses the surface of the soil to when it exits the container. This journey is not merely about the escape of excess water but about ensuring a harmonious balance that supports the plant's needs, allowing for adequate air flow to the roots, and preventing the buildup of harmful pathogens that thrive in stagnant, anaerobic conditions.

The challenge of ensuring proper drainage begins with the container selection, a narrative that weaves through the fabric of container gardening. The choice of material and design of the pot, the presence or absence of drainage holes, and the use of additional drainage aids are all chapters in the story of a plant's journey towards optimal health. Containers with inadequate drainage are akin to sealed chambers, where water accumulates at the bottom, creating an environment ripe for root rot, a silent killer that suffocates and drowns the roots in a pool of excess moisture.

Addressing the challenges of drainage requires innovation and a touch of gardening wisdom. The traditional solution has been the use of drainage holes, small gateways at the bottom of containers that allow water to escape. Yet, the narrative does not end here. The size and number of these holes must be carefully considered, too few or too small, and they become ineffective, too large, and they risk soil loss. It's a delicate balance, a dance between retaining enough moisture for the plant's needs and allowing excess water to freely exit the container.

The plot thickens with the introduction of materials placed at the bottom of pots to enhance drainage. Gravel, pebbles, and broken pieces of pottery have been protagonists in the story of drainage, creating a layer that water can filter through, slowing its journey and preventing soil from clogging the drainage holes. However, recent insights challenge this practice, suggesting that such layers might hinder rather than help water movement, creating an interface that traps water above the gravel layer, potentially exacerbating issues of waterlogging.

The innovative gardener turns to soil composition as a key player in the drainage drama. A well-structured potting mix, light and porous, becomes the ideal medium, facilitating water flow and root penetration. The incorporation of materials such as perlite, vermiculite, or coconut coir into the mix introduces a level of aeration and moisture retention that supports healthy root growth while ensuring that water does not stagnate. The narrative of drainage is also a tale of vigilance. Monitoring watering practices, being mindful of the weather, and understanding the water needs of each plant species are all critical elements of the story. Overwatering is a common misstep on the path to gardening success, a well-intentioned act that can lead to detrimental outcomes. The wise gardener knows that the soil should be allowed to dry slightly between waterings, a practice that encourages roots to grow stronger as they search for moisture, building a foundation for robust plant health.

In the grand garden of container gardening, drainage emerges as a fundamental principle, a core element that influences the health and vitality of the garden. It's a reflection of the gardener's dedication to creating an environment where plants can thrive, where the beauty of nature can be showcased in the heart of urban spaces, on patios, balconies, and beyond. The importance of drainage is a reminder of the delicate balance required to sustain life, a balance that, when respected and maintained, allows the container garden to flourish, bringing joy, beauty, and abundance to the gardener's world.

Benefits of Container Gardening

Container gardening, an art form as ancient as agriculture itself, has evolved into a vibrant thread in the tapestry of modern horticulture. This practice, which involves growing plants in containers instead of planting them in the ground, is not merely a solution for space constraints but a profound way to connect with nature, enhance living spaces, and cultivate well-being. The benefits of container gardening unfold in layers, revealing a depth that transcends the simple act of potting a plant.

At its core, container gardening offers unparalleled versatility. It allows the gardener to curate a personal oasis in the unlikeliest of places, from the sprawling balcony of an urban apartment to the sun-drenched patio of a suburban home. This flexibility to create green spaces in areas otherwise unsuitable for traditional gardening is a testament to the ingenuity and resilience of gardeners. Containers can be moved to capture the sun's changing path, to shelter plants from harsh weather, or to rearrange spaces for gatherings, making the garden an ever-evolving tapestry that reflects the rhythms of life and the seasons.

Moreover, container gardening democratizes the act of gardening, making it accessible to all, regardless of land ownership or soil quality. It opens the world of horticulture to those who might otherwise be excluded, providing a pathway for everyone to experience the joy and satisfaction of tending to plants. This inclusivity extends to educational settings, where container gardens become living classrooms, teaching young and old alike about the cycles of growth, the importance of care, and the impact of environmental stewardship.

The health benefits of container gardening are both tangible and subtle. On a physical level, the act of gardening engages the body, combining gentle exercise with the therapeutic touch of soil and plants. This connection to the earth has been shown to reduce stress, improve mood, and enhance mental well-being. The psychological uplift associated with tending to a garden, watching it grow and thrive under one's care, is a powerful antidote to the pressures of modern life. Moreover, container gardening can contribute to a healthier diet, with fresh herbs, vegetables, and fruits grown just steps from the kitchen door, enriching meals with flavors and nutrients straight from the garden.

Environmentally, container gardening represents a microcosm of sustainable practices. It encourages the use of organic methods, reduces the need for chemical fertilizers and pesticides, and can contribute to biodiversity by supporting a variety of plants, including native species and pollinators. The use of recycled containers and compost made from kitchen scraps closes the loop of waste, turning potential landfill into life-giving soil. This miniature model of sustainability serves as a daily reminder of the impact individual actions can have on the health of the planet.

Aesthetically, container gardens are a canvas for creativity. They allow for the exploration of color, form, and texture, blending the hues of flowers, the architecture of leaves, and the drama of varying heights and depths. This creative expression is not static; it evolves with the seasons, with the gardener's growing confidence and with the serendipitous discoveries of new plants and combinations. Container gardens can transform spaces, adding vibrancy to drab corners, softening hard lines, and inviting nature into the most industrial of environments.

Socially, container gardening fosters community. Shared balcony gardens, community gardening projects, and even social media groups dedicated to container gardening create bonds among individuals. These communities share knowledge, celebrate successes, and provide support through challenges, weaving a network of connections rooted in a shared love of gardening. This communal aspect of container gardening enriches lives, breaking down barriers of isolation and building bridges of understanding and friendship.

In essence, container gardening is a celebration of life's adaptability, creativity, and resilience. It is a practice that nurtures not only plants but the human spirit, offering solace, joy, and a deep connection to the natural world. The benefits of container gardening unfold in the quiet moments of morning watering, in the pride of the first harvest, and in the tranquil beauty of a garden bathed in the golden light of sunset. It is a testament to the power of plants to transform spaces and lives, a reminder of the simple pleasures and profound insights that gardening can bring.

Container gardening, with its myriad benefits, stands as a beacon of hope and beauty in a fast-paced world. It is a call to slow down, to nurture, and to celebrate the earth, even in the smallest of spaces. This practice, rooted in the ancient bond between humans and plants, continues to grow, enriched by each gardener's unique vision and the shared joy of creating life in containers.

Chapter 4: Plant Selection & Maintenance

Choosing the right plants for your climate and space is akin to casting characters for a play. Each plant, with its unique needs, strengths, and beauty, must fit perfectly into the role it's given, thriving under the spotlight of your garden's specific conditions. This careful selection process is fundamental, not just for the health and growth of your garden, but for its harmony and aesthetic appeal.

The journey of selecting the right plants begins with an understanding of your garden's climate zone. This knowledge acts as a compass, guiding you through the vast sea of plant varieties to those best suited to your garden's environmental conditions. Climate zones, defined by temperature extremes, length of growing season, and precipitation patterns, are the backdrop against which your garden's drama unfolds. Selecting plants adapted to your zone ensures they are well-prepared for the climatic challenges they will face, be it a scorching summer sun or the chill of frosty nights.

Equally important is the understanding of microclimates within your garden. Even within a small space, variations in elevation, proximity to buildings or water bodies, and exposure to sun and wind can create pockets of different growing conditions. A plant that thrives in the sunny warmth of your garden's southern edge might languish in the cooler, shadowed northern side. Observing these subtle differences and choosing plants that match the microclimates in your garden is like fitting puzzle pieces together, each plant in its perfect place, contributing to the overall picture of beauty and abundance.

The size and structure of your garden space also play crucial roles in plant selection. A sprawling backyard offers a canvas for larger specimens, fruit trees, and expansive vegetable gardens, while a cozy balcony or small patio might call for compact, container-friendly varieties. Vertical gardening techniques, such as trellises and wall planters, can expand your options, allowing you to grow climbers and vine plants, thus maximizing the use of limited space. This spatial awareness ensures that each plant not only fits physically but also contributes to the desired aesthetic and functional goals of your garden. Beyond environmental and spatial considerations, choosing plants for your garden is also a matter of personal preference and goals. Are you seeking to create a culinary garden, rich with herbs and vegetables for your table? Or is your vision one of beauty and fragrance, a floral haven that delights the senses? Perhaps your aim is to support local wildlife, planting native species that offer food and shelter for birds, bees, and butterflies. Understanding your gardening goals helps to narrow down the plant selection, ensuring that each addition to your garden serves a purpose and brings you closer to the vision you have in mind.

Maintenance requirements are another critical factor in plant selection. Each plant comes with its own set of needs in terms of watering, feeding, pruning, and pest management. Selecting plants with similar care requirements can simplify garden maintenance, creating a more harmonious relationship between you and your garden. It's important to be realistic about the time and resources you can dedicate to garden care, choosing plants that fit within those constraints to ensure a healthy and thriving garden.

The process of choosing the right plants for your climate and space is a thoughtful and creative endeavor, a blend of science, art, and personal expression. It requires research, observation, and sometimes a bit of trial and error. Garden centers, local nurseries, and gardening communities can be invaluable resources, offering advice, inspiration, and the plants themselves, each with a story and potential waiting to be unlocked in your garden.

In cultivating life in your garden, remember that each plant selection is a step towards creating a living ecosystem, a space that nurtures and sustains both the plants and the gardener. It's a dynamic process, one that evolves with time, experience, and the changing seasons. With each plant carefully chosen for your climate and space, you weave a tapestry of life that reflects the diversity and beauty of the natural world, a personal sanctuary that grows more precious with each passing year. Selecting the right plants is the heart of gardening, a practice that connects us to the earth and to the cycles of life. It's an act of hope and optimism, planting a seed or a young sapling with the belief in its potential to grow and flourish. This connection, this act of cultivation, is what transforms a collection of plants into a garden, and a gardener into a steward of the living world.

A Care Guide for Common Plants

Tending to a garden is akin to orchestrating a symphony, where each plant plays a unique role, contributing its beauty and vitality to the collective harmony of the space. The care guide for common plants is a comprehensive manual that assists gardeners in nurturing their living ensemble, ensuring each member thrives. This guide delves into the art and science of plant care, weaving together knowledge, intuition, and a deep connection to the natural world.

At the heart of plant care lies the understanding of each plant's specific needs—water, light, soil, and nutrients being the fundamental elements that sustain life. Water, the source of life for all living beings, demands attention and wisdom in its application to plants. Each species has its unique hydration needs, with some thriving in moist soils and others preferring drier conditions. Overwatering is as much a peril as underwatering, leading to root rot or dehydration. The key is to observe the plant's behavior, letting the soil's moisture level guide your watering routine, ensuring that each plant receives just the right amount of water to flourish.

Light, the energy source for the miraculous process of photosynthesis, varies widely in its necessity among different plants. While some plants bask in the full glory of the sun, others thrive under the gentle caress of dappled shade. Understanding the light requirements of each plant is crucial, positioning them in your garden or home where they receive the optimal intensity and duration of light. This might mean placing sun-lovers near south-facing windows or in the open garden and finding cooler, shaded spots for those that favor less direct exposure.

Soil quality and composition form the foundation of plant health, offering support, nutrients, and oxygen to roots. Each plant species has its preferences for soil pH, texture, and nutrient content. Amending your garden soil with compost, peat moss, or other organic materials can improve its structure, fertility, and water-holding capacity, catering to the diverse needs of your plant collection. Regular testing of soil pH and nutrient levels can guide your amendments, creating a fertile ground for your plants to grow.

Nutrition is another pillar of plant care, with each species having its dietary preferences. While some plants are heavy feeders, requiring frequent fertilization, others thrive in leaner soils with minimal supplemental nutrients. Choosing the right fertilizer—be it organic or synthetic—its formulation, and understanding the appropriate application rates and timing are essential practices that bolster plant health and productivity.

Beyond these basics, pest and disease management is an integral part of plant care, requiring vigilance and a proactive approach. Regular inspections of your plants for signs of distress, pests, or disease can catch problems early, making them easier to manage. Integrating pest and disease-resistant varieties, practicing crop rotation, and employing natural predators and barriers can help maintain a healthy garden ecosystem.

Pruning and grooming, though often overlooked, are vital care practices that shape the plant's growth, encourage flowering and fruiting, and remove diseased or damaged tissues. These practices not only enhance the plant's appearance but also improve its health and vitality, encouraging a more robust and productive growth. The care guide for common plants is not merely a set of instructions; it's a dynamic dialogue between the gardener and their plants. It requires observation, adaptation, and a willingness to learn from each season's successes and setbacks. This guide serves as a compass, pointing gardeners toward practices that align with the rhythms of nature and the needs of their plant companions.

In cultivating a garden, we engage in an act of co-creation with nature, a partnership where care and attention are rewarded with the unfurling of leaves, the blossoming of flowers, and the bounty of fruits and vegetables. This guide is a testament to the gardener's role as both caretaker and student, continually learning from the plants and the environment, adapting care practices to meet the ever-changing conditions of the garden.

Gardening, at its essence, is an expression of love for the natural world, a pursuit that nourishes not just the body with its harvests but the soul with its beauty and tranquility. The care guide for common plants is a beacon for this journey, illuminating the path to a thriving garden where life, in its myriad forms, is celebrated and cherished.

Planting and Harvesting Calendar: The Gardener's Almanac

In the heart of every gardener beats a rhythm, a pulse that aligns with the cycles of the earth—the seasonal ebb and flow that dictates the life cycle of plants. This rhythm is encapsulated in the planting and harvesting calendar, a gardener's almanac that guides the orchestration of sowing and reaping, ensuring that each plant is nurtured in harmony with the natural order.

The planting and harvesting calendar is not merely a schedule; it is a map of time, charting the course through the gardening year. It recognizes the subtle shifts in daylight, the gradual changes in temperature, and the deep, underlying currents of the earth's fertility cycles. This calendar is the gardener's compass, pointing the way to successful cultivation by aligning garden activities with the optimal conditions for plant growth.

Understanding the calendar begins with the recognition of frost dates—those critical milestones that mark the safe passage from the dormancy of winter to the growth season of spring, and again, the transition as summer wanes into the rest of autumn. These dates define the window for planting, a period when the soil has warmed enough to welcome seeds and tender seedlings, free from the threat of a killing frost.

For each crop, there is a time to sow—some seeds stir beneath the soil as the first thaw of late winter loosens the earth's grip, while others wait until the warmth of late spring caresses the land. The calendar takes into account the life cycle of each plant, the days to germination, and the journey to maturity, ensuring that each is sown at the precise moment that nature intended. This timing is crucial, as planting too early or too late can disrupt the plant's natural development, leading to poor yields or failure to thrive.

The rhythm of the calendar is not uniform; it varies by region, influenced by the local climate and the specific conditions of each garden. Adjusting the calendar to fit your garden's microclimate, taking into account variations in elevation, exposure, and proximity to bodies of water, fine-tunes the timing of planting and harvesting, tailoring it to the unique environment of your garden.

A planting and harvesting calendar also embrace succession planting, a technique that extends the harvest season by staggering plantings of certain crops at regular intervals. This method ensures a continuous supply of fresh vegetables and herbs, maximizing the productivity of the garden space and extending the joy of harvesting.

Month	Planting Activities	Harvesting Activities
January	- Start indoor seedlings for spring planting (e.g., tomatoes, peppers).	- Harvest winter crops in mild climates (e.g., kale, collards).
February	- Continue starting seeds indoors. - Prepare beds as weather permits.	- Harvest winter crops as available.

Month	Planting Activities	Harvesting Activities
March	- Plant early spring crops outdoors (e.g., peas, spinach, lettuce). - Transplant seedlings indoors for later transplant.	- Begin harvesting early spring crops.
April	- Plant root crops (e.g., carrots, beets). - Plant potatoes. - Continue transplanting seedlings outdoors.	- Harvest spring crops.
May	- Plant warm-season crops after the last frost (e.g., tomatoes, corn, beans).	- Harvest late spring crops.
June	- Plant second crops of fast-growing vegetables (e.g., radishes, lettuce).	- Harvest early summer crops (e.g., strawberries, peas).
July	- Start fall crops indoors. - Continue planting fast-growing, heat-loving vegetables.	- Harvest mid-summer crops (e.g., tomatoes, cucumbers).
August	- Begin transplanting fall	- Harvest late summer crops.

Month	Planting Activities	Harvesting Activities
	crops outdoors. - Direct sow fall crops (e.g., kale, turnips).	- Begin harvesting early-planted fall crops.
September	- Continue transplanting and direct sowing fall crops.	- Harvest peak summer crops. - Continue harvesting fall crops.
October	- Plant garlic for next year. - Prepare and protect fall crops for cooler nights.	- Harvest fall crops. - Collect seeds for next year.
November	- Plant cover crops in empty beds. - Clean up garden beds and compost plant debris.	- Finish harvesting late fall crops before first frost.
December	- Plan next year's garden. - Order seeds and garden supplies.	- Harvest remaining winter-hardy crops.

Moreover, the calendar is a record of the garden's life, a journal that captures the ebb and flow of the seasons. It notes the first bloom of spring, the peak of summer's bounty, and the last harvest before the frost. This record, kept from year to year, becomes a repository of knowledge, capturing observations, successes, and lessons learned. It guides future plantings, helping to refine the rhythm of the garden with each passing season. The art of creating and following a planting and harvesting calendar is a dance with time, a partnership between the gardener and the natural world. It requires attentiveness to the subtleties of the changing seasons, a willingness to learn from the land, and the flexibility to adapt to nature's cues.

In this dance, the gardener becomes attuned to the deeper rhythms of life, finding joy in the anticipation of the first sprouts of spring, the abundance of the summer harvest, and the satisfaction of preparing the garden for its winter rest. The calendar is a testament to the cyclical nature of life, a reminder that in gardening, as in life, there is a time for every purpose under the sun.

Crafting a planting and harvesting calendar is an act of hope and optimism, a declaration of faith in the future. It is a reflection of the gardener's commitment to stewardship of the earth, a careful planning that ensures not just the survival, but the thriving of the garden. This calendar is more than a tool; it is a narrative of growth, a story of life cultivated with care, patience, and respect for the rhythms of the earth.

Chapter 5: Soil Science: Creating a Fertile Foundation

Creating and maintaining fertile soil

Creating and maintaining fertile soil is an art form that dates back to the very inception of agriculture, a practice refined and revered through generations of farmers, gardeners, and caretakers of the earth. It's a foundational element of gardening that transcends mere dirt or substrate, embodying the very essence of life and growth. Fertile soil is not just about the ability to support plant life; it's about creating a living, breathing ecosystem that sustains and nurtures a diverse array of organisms, contributing to the health and well-being of the planet.

At the heart of fertile soil lies its structure, a delicate balance between sand, silt, and clay. This balance, known as soil texture, determines the soil's ability to hold water and nutrients, to breathe, and to offer a home to countless microorganisms that form the backbone of the garden's ecosystem. Creating and maintaining this balance is akin to crafting a masterpiece, requiring knowledge, patience, and a deep respect for the natural world.

Organic matter is the soul of fertile soil. It's the decomposed remnants of plants and animals, transformed through time and the tireless work of microorganisms into humus, the dark, nutrient-rich heart of the soil. Incorporating organic matter into the soil is a practice as old as agriculture itself, a way to return to the earth what has been taken, closing a cycle that nourishes life. This addition improves soil structure, enhances water retention, and feeds the microscopic lifeforms that, in turn, feed the plants.

The introduction of compost into the garden is a testament to the gardener's commitment to sustainability and regeneration. Compost, the black gold of the garden, is created from the remnants of kitchen scraps, yard waste, and other organic materials, transformed through the alchemy of decomposition into a substance rich in nutrients and life. This process, both simple and complex, mirrors the cycles of nature, turning waste into wealth, and feeding the soil as the soil feeds the plants.

But creating fertile soil is not just about what we add; it's also about what we do not take away. The practice of cover cropping, for instance, protects the soil from erosion, adds organic matter, and fixes nitrogen, enriching the soil without the need for chemical fertilizers. Crop rotation, another age-old practice, prevents the depletion of specific nutrients, reducing the need for external inputs and keeping the soil vibrant and alive.

Water management, too, plays a crucial role in maintaining soil fertility. The right amount of water, delivered at the right time, ensures that plants have the moisture they need without drowning the soil's microorganisms or washing away vital nutrients. Mulching, with its dual ability to retain moisture and add organic matter, is a simple yet effective tool in the gardener's arsenal, protecting the soil while contributing to its ongoing fertility.

The magic of fertile soil lies not just in its physical attributes but in its life. A teaspoon of fertile soil can contain billions of bacteria, fungi, protozoa, and other microorganisms, each playing a role in the garden's ecosystem. These microscopic lifeforms are the unsung heroes of the soil, breaking down organic matter, fixing nitrogen, and creating the complex web of life that supports plant growth. Nurturing this soil life is as important as any nutrient we might add, for it is these organisms that transform dead matter into living soil, turning the soil into a dynamic entity capable of supporting life in all its forms.

Maintaining fertile soil is a continuous process, a dialogue between the gardener and the garden. It requires observation, intervention, and, most importantly, a willingness to learn and adapt. Soil fertility can be diminished by overuse, pollution, and neglect, but with care and respect, it can be restored and even enhanced. This process of creation and maintenance is not just a technical challenge; it's a philosophical and ethical commitment to stewardship of the land, to a way of gardening that respects the interconnectedness of all life.

In the end, creating and maintaining fertile soil is about more than just plants; it's about creating a foundation for a healthy ecosystem, a sustainable future, and a connection to the earth that nourishes both body and soul. It's a testament to the power of care, attention, and respect for the natural world, principles that guide not just the creation of fertile soil but the very essence of gardening itself.

Composting and Natural Fertilizers: The Lifeblood of the Garden

In the realm of soil science, the practice of composting and the application of natural fertilizers stand as testament to the gardener's alchemy, a transformative process turning the ordinary into the extraordinary. This art form, rooted in the ancient wisdom of the earth's cycles, revitalizes the soil, rekindling its life force and enhancing its fertility without the reliance on synthetic interventions. It's a celebration of nature's resilience and bounty, an acknowledgment that in the detritus of life lies the potential for rebirth and renewal.

Composting, at its core, is the process of facilitating decay, of overseeing the transformation of organic waste into nutrient-rich humus. This dark, crumbly, earth-scented matter is the gold standard of garden soil amendments, teeming with microorganisms and replete with the nutrients plants crave. The compost pile is a microcosm of the ecosystem at work, a bustling metropolis of bacteria, fungi, worms, and insects, each playing a role in breaking down the raw materials into their elemental forms.

The beauty of composting lies in its simplicity and its sustainability. Kitchen scraps, lawn clippings, leaves, and even paper products are reborn, given a second life as the foundation of garden health. This cycle of renewal not only reduces waste but enriches the soil, closing a loop that sustains the garden's productivity year after year. Composting teaches us patience and respect for the natural processes, reminding us that time and nature work hand in hand to create something of value from what is often overlooked and discarded. Natural fertilizers, derived from plant, animal, and mineral sources, complement the practice of composting by providing targeted nutrition to the soil. Unlike their synthetic counterparts, these fertilizers offer a slow release of nutrients, mimicking the natural feeding rhythms of plants. They nourish not just the plants but the soil itself, enhancing its structure, encouraging the proliferation of beneficial microorganisms, and maintaining a balance that supports a diverse ecosystem.

The application of natural fertilizers such as bone meal, blood meal, fish emulsion, and green manure is both a science and an art. It requires an understanding of the soil's current state and the specific needs of the plants it nurtures. Each natural fertilizer brings its unique profile of nutrients, from the phosphorus-rich bone meal that stimulates root development to the nitrogen-laden blood meal that fuels leafy growth. Green manures, cover crops grown to be plowed back into the soil, enrich the earth with organic matter and nutrients, improving soil structure and fertility.

The integration of composting and natural fertilizers into the garden's regimen is a declaration of independence from chemical inputs, a commitment to gardening in a manner that honors the earth's natural cycles and processes. It's an approach that values longevity over immediacy, quality over quantity, recognizing that true fertility is not just about the abundance of harvest but the health of the soil that sustains it.

This philosophy extends beyond the practical benefits to the soil and plants. It reflects a broader understanding of our place within the natural world, a recognition that our actions in the garden ripple through the ecosystem. Composting and the use of natural fertilizers are acts of stewardship, ways of giving back to the earth that sustains us, ensuring that the soil, that thin crust of the planet that teems with life, remains vibrant and fertile for generations to come.

In adopting these practices, we align ourselves with the forces of growth and decay that drive the natural world, participating in a cycle that is as old as life itself. We become conduits through which waste is transformed into wealth, decay into growth, and death into life. This is the essence of composting and natural fertilizers, a deep, enduring connection to the lifeblood of the garden, a commitment to nurturing the soil that, in turn, nurtures us.

Soil testing and pH adjustment

Embarking on the journey of soil testing and pH adjustment is akin to unlocking the secret language of the earth beneath our feet. This process is not merely a scientific endeavor but a deep communion with the land, an act of listening and responding to the subtle cues and whispers of the soil. It's an essential chapter in the gardener's quest to create and maintain a fertile foundation, a harmonious environment where plants can thrive.

Soil testing, at its heart, is an exploration, a quest to uncover the hidden complexities of the soil's composition. It's a way of peering beneath the surface, beyond what the eye can see, to understand the myriad elements that influence plant health and growth. This exploration begins with the simple act of gathering soil samples, a mosaic of the garden's diversity, each with its story, its history, and its potential. The act of testing these samples, whether through home kits or professional laboratories, reveals the soil's secrets—its pH, nutrient levels, organic matter content, and more. This information is a treasure trove, a map that guides the gardener's hand in nurturing the soil. The pH level, in particular, is a critical piece of this puzzle. It's a measure of the soil's acidity or alkalinity, a scale that influences the availability of nutrients to plants, their ability to take root, and flourish.

Adjusting the pH of the soil is an art, a delicate balance that respects the natural equilibrium of the earth while gently nudging it towards the ideal conditions for plant life. For soils too acidic, the addition of lime can raise the pH, unlocking nutrients bound in the earth and fostering a more hospitable environment for a wide array of plants. Conversely, for soils that lean towards alkalinity, sulfur can lower the pH, creating conditions favored by acid-loving species, enriching the tapestry of the garden with a diversity of life.

This dance of adjustment, of adding and amending, is not a once-off performance but a continuous dialogue with the land. It requires patience, observation, and a willingness to learn from the outcomes of each intervention. The soil responds to these adjustments over time, revealing its changes in the vigor of the plants, the brightness of their leaves, and the abundance of their flowers and fruits. Beyond the science, soil testing, and pH adjustment are acts of care, of stewardship. They reflect a commitment to the health of the garden ecosystem, a recognition that fertile soil is the foundation upon which all life in the garden depends. It's a practice that ties the gardener to generations past and future, a thread in the fabric of an ancient tradition of cultivation and care for the earth.

In this process, the gardener becomes a student of the land, learning its rhythms, its needs, and its language. This knowledge is empowering, transforming gardening from a series of trials and errors into an informed practice, guided by the understanding of the soil's inner workings. It's a journey that deepens the connection between the gardener and the garden, grounding the act of cultivation in the science and soul of soil stewardship.

The narrative of soil testing and pH adjustment is woven with threads of humility and wonder, a story that celebrates the complexity and richness of the soil. It's a reminder that, in gardening, we are not just shaping the land but being shaped by it, taught by the earth as we seek to nurture and sustain it. This chapter in the gardener's guide is a testament to the beauty and depth of the gardening endeavor, a pursuit that merges knowledge with passion, science with art, and work with wonder.

As the seasons turn and the garden grows, the practice of soil testing and pH adjustment remains a cornerstone of garden health, a ritual that honors the dynamic, ever-changing nature of the soil. It's a commitment to the land that yields not just bountiful harvests but a deeper understanding of the life beneath our feet, an appreciation for the delicate balance that sustains all living things.

In embracing this practice, gardeners forge a bond with the earth, a partnership that nurtures not just plants but the human spirit. It's a journey of discovery, a path that leads to a fertile foundation for the garden and the soul, grounded in the science and magic of the soil.

Chapter 6: The Art of Watering: Irrigation Strategies

Do-it-yourself irrigation systems

Embarking on the journey of crafting do-it-yourself irrigation systems is akin to weaving a tapestry of life-giving water throughout the garden. This endeavor, rooted in the ancient wisdom of agriculture and infused with the ingenuity of modern gardening, represents a harmonious blend of art and science. It's a testament to the gardener's commitment to nurturing the land, a sustainable approach that ensures every drop of water serves the purpose of fostering growth and vitality in the garden.

The art of DIY irrigation begins with understanding the unique needs of your garden, recognizing that each plant, each row, and each plot has its own thirst to quench. This understanding lays the groundwork for a system that is both efficient and elegant, tailored to the rhythms of nature and the specifics of your soil, climate, and crop types. It's about creating a symphony of water delivery, where every nozzle, drip emitter, and hose is an instrument in the orchestra of irrigation, playing its part to sustain the garden. t the heart of the DIY irrigation approach is the principle of delivering water directly to where it's most needed—the roots. Drip irrigation systems embody this principle, transforming the way water is delivered by minimizing waste and maximizing efficiency. Constructing such a system can be a simple endeavor, involving little more than a series of hoses punctuated by drip emitters or soaker hoses laid out beneath the canopy of leaves. This setup ensures that water seeps slowly into the soil, reaching the roots without the excess that leads to runoff or evaporation.

The innovation of the gardener shines in the adaptation of household items to serve in these irrigation systems. Recycled plastic bottles, punctured with tiny holes and buried next to plants, can become reservoirs that slowly release water into the soil. PVC pipes, rigged with strategically drilled holes and connected to a water source, can irrigate rows of crops with precision. Even old garden hoses can be repurposed into effective soaker hoses, providing a steady, gentle flow of water to thirsty plants.

Beyond the mechanics, the DIY irrigation system is a reflection of the gardener's relationship with the environment. Rain barrels positioned to catch runoff from rooftops can supply water to the garden, embodying the principles of conservation and sustainability. Timers and moisture sensors, integrated into the irrigation setup, ensure that water is used judiciously, only when the plants demand it, and never in excess. This careful management of resources is a dance with the natural world, a balance of giving and taking that sustains the garden and conserves the precious resource of water. The creation of a DIY irrigation system is more than a practical task; it's a journey into the heart of gardening itself. It requires creativity, patience, and a willingness to experiment and learn from both successes and setbacks. Each garden is a living laboratory, where the principles of irrigation are tested and refined, adapted to the ever-changing conditions of the weather, the soil, and the cycles of plant life.

This endeavor is also a statement of independence, a declaration that the gardener is not reliant on costly, complex systems to sustain their crops. Instead, with a few simple materials and a deep understanding of their garden's needs, they can create an irrigation system that is both effective and deeply personal. It's a testament to the power of human ingenuity to work in harmony with nature, to sustain and nurture life with the simple element of water.

In embracing the art of DIY irrigation, the gardener becomes a steward of the land, an architect of abundance who understands that the right amount of water, delivered in the right way, can turn a patch of earth into a thriving garden. This system, built with care and foresight, becomes an integral part of the garden's ecosystem, supporting life during the heat of summer, the dry spells of autumn, and all the seasons of the garden's life.

The journey of creating and implementing a DIY irrigation system is a profound act of connection with the natural world, a way of gardening that is as rewarding as it is effective. It's a path that leads to lush growth, bountiful harvests, and the deep satisfaction of knowing that every drop of water is used wisely, every plant nurtured with precision. This is the essence of the DIY approach to irrigation, a blend of art, science, and deep ecological awareness that enriches the garden and the gardener alike.

Frequency and quantity of watering

Understanding the frequency and quantity of watering in the garden is akin to learning the language of plants, a delicate dance between giving and withholding, that when mastered, leads to a garden that is both vibrant and resilient. This dance is not led by the gardener but by the garden itself, with each plant whispering its needs through the curl of a leaf, the droop of a stem, or the vibrancy of its growth.

Watering, at its core, is an act of attentiveness—a responsive, intuitive process that goes beyond mere schedules to a deeper understanding of the garden's unique rhythms. The frequency of watering is not dictated by the calendar but by the soil's moisture content, the weather, and the plant's lifecycle. It's a rhythm that changes with the seasons, with the waxing and waning of the moon, and with the shifting patterns of the climate.

In the heart of summer, when the sun reigns supreme and the earth bakes under its gaze, the frequency of watering must rise to meet the increased demand. Here, the early morning becomes a sacred time, a moment of communion between the gardener and the garden, as water is delivered to quench the night's thirst. Yet, as autumn approaches, with its cooler days and chilly nights, the garden's thirst diminishes, and the frequency of watering adjusts to this new rhythm, a reflection of the garden's changing needs.

The quantity of water, too, is a matter of precision and balance. Too much water, and the plants drown, starved of oxygen and vulnerable to rot; too little, and they wither, unable to draw the nutrients they need from the soil. Here, the gardener must become a student of their garden, learning to read the signs of thirst and satiety in their plants, understanding that each species, each variety, has its own unique requirements.

This knowledge is not innate but cultivated through observation, experimentation, and the wisdom passed down from one generation of gardeners to the next. It's a knowledge that recognizes the importance of deep watering, encouraging roots to grow downward in search of moisture, building a foundation of strength and stability for the plant. It eschews the superficiality of frequent, shallow watering, which leads to weak root systems and plants that are dependent on the gardener's constant attention.

Incorporating mulch into the garden's irrigation strategy is a testament to the gardener's understanding of water's value. Mulch acts as a blanket, conserving moisture, reducing evaporation, and maintaining a consistent soil temperature. This layer of protection allows the gardener to water less frequently, yet more effectively, ensuring that each drop of water is used to its fullest potential.

The art of watering is also a science, grounded in the understanding of soil types and their water-holding capacities, the evapotranspiration rates of plants, and the microclimates within the garden. It requires tools— not just hoses and watering cans, but moisture meters, mulch, and the knowledge of how to use them effectively. It's a dynamic, responsive approach that adapts to the immediate conditions of the garden, informed by both data and intuition.

Mastering the frequency and quantity of watering is an ongoing journey, a process of continual learning and adaptation. It's a practice that fosters a deep, enduring connection between the gardener and the garden, a dialogue that nurtures not just the plants but the soul of the gardener. In this dance of water, the gardener learns the rhythms of life, the ebb and flow of growth and rest, and the joy of seeing their garden flourish under their careful, attentive hand.

This exploration of watering practices is a call to gardeners to listen to their gardens, to observe, respond, and adapt to the changing needs of their plants. It's an invitation to engage in a practice that is both ancient and urgently contemporary, a practice that lies at the heart of sustainable gardening and the stewardship of our planet's precious resources. In mastering the art and science of watering, gardeners play a vital role in the cycle of life, sustaining the beauty and abundance of the earth one garden at a time.

Water conservation and rainwater harvesting

In the garden, water is more than a resource; it is the lifeblood that sustains every leaf, petal, and root. Yet, as gardeners, our stewardship extends beyond the soil to the very essence of sustainability—conserving this precious element while nurturing the earth. The ancient practice of rainwater harvesting, coupled with modern water conservation techniques, forms a symbiotic relationship with the environment, a pact between the gardener and the natural world that promises mutual respect and care.

Rainwater harvesting is an alchemy of sorts, a method that transforms the ephemeral into the enduring, capturing the rain's transient bounty so it may sustain life long after the clouds have passed. This practice, as old as agriculture itself, has been refined through the ages, evolving from simple catchment systems to sophisticated networks of barrels, tanks, and reservoirs. These systems, whether DIY constructs fashioned from repurposed materials or commercially available solutions, are testament to the gardener's ingenuity and commitment to sustainability.

The beauty of rainwater harvesting lies not just in its utility but in its simplicity. Rooftops become catchments, gutters transform into conduits, and barrels and tanks serve as sanctuaries of sustenance for the garden. This captured rainwater, free from the salts and chemicals often found in municipal water supplies, offers plants a taste of the sky, a nourishment that is both pure and profound.

Yet, the art of water conservation extends beyond harvesting rain. It encompasses a philosophy of mindfulness and efficiency, of making every drop count. Mulching, with its dual capacity to retain soil moisture and suppress weeds, is a prime example of this philosophy in action. So, too, is the practice of choosing drought-resistant plants, varieties that thrive on scant moisture, their roots drawing life from deep within the earth.

The integration of drip irrigation into this conservation ethos represents the pinnacle of efficiency. By delivering water directly to the roots, where it is most needed, drip systems minimize waste, reduce evaporation, and ensure that the precious resource of water is utilized with precision and care. Coupled with timers and moisture sensors, these systems embody the gardener's role as a guardian of the earth's resources, optimizing water use without sacrificing the vitality of the garden.

Water conservation and rainwater harvesting also reflect a broader awareness of the garden's place within the ecosystem. By reducing runoff, these practices mitigate erosion and the leaching of nutrients, preserving the integrity of both the garden and the surrounding landscape. They contribute to the health of local waterways, reducing the burden on stormwater systems and fostering a healthier, more resilient environment.

This holistic approach to water management—rooted in respect for the natural world and a commitment to sustainability—is a powerful act of creation. It transforms the garden into a microcosm of ecological balance, a place where human ingenuity and nature's bounty coalesce in harmony. The garden becomes a model of environmental stewardship, a testament to the possibility of a sustainable future nurtured by the hands of mindful gardeners.

Embarking on the journey of water conservation and rainwater harvesting is to engage in a dialogue with the elements, to listen to the whispers of rain and respond with gratitude and care. It is to recognize that in every drop of water lies the potential for growth, renewal, and life. This practice is an invitation to gardeners to become alchemists of the modern age, transforming the simple act of watering into a sacred stewardship of the earth's most precious resource.

In this narrative of conservation and harvesting, we find more than techniques and strategies; we discover a path to deeper connection with our gardens and the world around us. It is a path paved with the knowledge that through our actions, we can sustain not just the plants in our care but the planet that sustains us all. Water conservation and rainwater harvesting are not just acts of gardening; they are acts of hope, a commitment to a future where gardens and gardeners play a vital role in the stewardship of our earth.

Chapter 7: Managing Pests and Diseases

Ecological identification and treatment

In the heart of every garden lies an intricate web of life, a delicate balance between growth and decay, health and disease, abundance and scarcity. Navigating this complex ecosystem requires more than just a keen eye and a ready hand; it demands an understanding of the garden as a living entity, where every leaf, stem, and root plays a role in the broader environmental tapestry. The ecological identification and treatment of pests and diseases is not merely a method of garden management; it is an ethos, a way of interacting with the natural world that is both respectful and responsive.

The journey begins with observation, a deep and attentive engagement with the garden that goes beyond casual glances to a thoughtful examination of the signs and symptoms presented by plants. This is the first step in ecological identification, a process that seeks to understand not just the presence of a pest or disease but its role within the garden ecosystem. It's an approach that acknowledges the garden as a microcosm of the wider world, where every organism, whether deemed beneficial or pestilential, has a part to play.

Understanding the life cycles of common garden pests and diseases forms the foundation of this ecological approach. It's a knowledge that spans the seasons, recognizing the times of year when certain pests are most active or when diseases are likely to spread. This temporal awareness is crucial, allowing the gardener to anticipate challenges and act proactively, rather than reactively, to maintain the balance of the garden.

Identification goes hand in hand with treatment, but in the ecological garden, treatment is not synonymous with eradication. Instead, it's about management and balance, employing strategies that minimize harm to the garden's beneficial inhabitants while curbing the impact of those less welcome. It's a nuanced approach that favors diversity over monoculture, interplanting and companion planting over chemical reliance, encouraging a garden that is resilient in the face of adversity.

Biological control plays a pivotal role in this ecological strategy, leveraging the natural relationships between organisms to manage pest populations. Introducing or encouraging the presence of beneficial insects, such as ladybugs to combat aphids or parasitic wasps to check caterpillar populations, is a testament to the gardener's role as steward rather than conqueror. This method not only addresses the immediate challenge of pests but does so in a way that enhances the garden's biodiversity and ecological health.

Cultural practices, too, are integral to the ecological management of pests and diseases. Crop rotation, proper spacing, and sanitation reduce the habitat and resources available to pests, while increasing the vigor of plants, making them less susceptible to disease. These practices, rooted in the wisdom of generations, underscore the importance of working with, rather than against, the natural rhythms and conditions of the garden. The ecological identification and treatment of pests and diseases also embrace the use of organic and natural remedies, solutions that are gentle on the garden and its inhabitants but effective against unwanted guests. Neem oil, diatomaceous earth, and homemade insecticidal soaps are but a few of the tools in the ecological gardener's arsenal, each employed with consideration for its impact on the garden ecosystem.

This approach to managing pests and diseases is a reflection of a deeper philosophy, one that views the garden not as a static entity to be controlled but as a dynamic, living system. It's an acknowledgment that true health is not the absence of pests or diseases but the presence of balance, a harmony between the garden and the myriad forms of life it supports.

In adopting ecological identification and treatment methods, the gardener becomes a participant in this living system, a curator of balance and health. It's a role that requires patience, humility, and a willingness to learn from both successes and failures. But the rewards are immense, manifesting not just in the health of the plants but in the vibrancy of the garden ecosystem, a testament to the resilience and abundance that is possible when we choose to work in harmony with nature.

Prevention through garden design

In the world of gardening, the design of a garden is more than an aesthetic choice; it is a foundational strategy in the battle against pests and diseases. This approach transcends the traditional reliance on reactive measures, embracing instead a philosophy of prevention through thoughtful, intentional design. It's a testament to the gardener's foresight and understanding of the intricate web of life that thrives within the garden's borders.

At the heart of this strategy lies the principle of diversity. A garden rich in variety is a garden resilient in the face of adversity. By incorporating a wide range of plant species, the gardener creates a complex ecosystem that supports a balance of organisms, reducing the likelihood of any one pest or disease becoming dominant. This biodiversity is not just about the number of different plants, but their relationships to each other, to the soil, and to the myriad of creatures that call the garden home.

Companion planting is a practice that epitomizes this approach. By carefully selecting and positioning plants that offer mutual benefits—whether through pest deterrence, improved pollination, or enhanced nutrient uptake—the gardener weaves a tapestry of interdependence. Marigolds repel nematodes and attract beneficial insects, while basil planted near tomatoes may improve their flavor and deter pests. This method of design is both an art and a science, requiring knowledge of plant interactions and a creative vision for the garden's layout.

The strategic use of space and the physical structure of the garden also play crucial roles in preventing pests and diseases. Raised beds and well-defined pathways can improve air circulation and soil drainage, reducing the risk of fungal infections. The orientation of rows, the spacing between plants, and the direction of prevailing winds can all influence the garden's microclimate, making it more or less hospitable to potential invaders.

Incorporating natural barriers and physical deterrents is another facet of garden design with preventative power.

Hedgerows, netting, and even certain types of mulch can provide physical barriers against pests, while also enhancing the garden's aesthetic and ecological diversity. These elements can be strategically placed to protect more vulnerable plants or to create buffer zones that reduce the spread of diseases.

Water management, too, is integral to a preventative garden design. The placement of irrigation systems, the choice of watering methods, and the timing of water application can all influence the health of plants. Drip irrigation and soaker hoses, for example, deliver water directly to the soil, minimizing leaf wetness and the associated risk of fungal diseases. The design of the garden should facilitate these practices, ensuring that water is a source of life, not a vector for disease.

At its core, the philosophy of prevention through garden design is a reflection of the gardener's deep respect for nature and their role as a steward of the land. It's an acknowledgment that each choice, from the selection of plants to the layout of the garden, has implications for the health and harmony of the ecosystem. This approach requires patience, observation, and a willingness to learn and adapt over time. It's a dynamic process, one that evolves with each season, each new plant, and each challenge faced.

The garden designed with prevention in mind is a garden that thrives. It's a place of beauty and abundance, where pests and diseases are managed not with chemicals and interventions, but with foresight, diversity, and balance. This garden is a testament to the possibility of coexistence, a demonstration of how human ingenuity can align with natural processes to create a space that nourishes both the body and the soul.

In embracing this approach, the gardener becomes a composer of a living symphony, each element of the design a note in a harmonious score. The result is a garden that sings with life, a garden that is resilient, sustainable, and deeply connected to the web of life that sustains us all. This is the essence of prevention through garden design, a philosophy that sees the garden not as a collection of individual plants, but as a living, breathing ecosystem, a microcosm of the world we wish to see.

This exploration into the use of garden design as a preventative strategy against pests and diseases highlights the importance of foresight, diversity, and ecological balance. It illustrates how a thoughtful approach to garden layout and plant selection can serve as a fundamental pillar in maintaining garden health, embodying a deep respect for the intricate relationships that define the natural world.

Natural and safe remedies

In the garden, where life burgeons in every leaf and root, the presence of pests and diseases is a natural counterpart to growth. Yet, in this space where the cycles of life unfold, the wisdom to nurture and protect lies not in the harsh interventions of synthetic chemicals but in the gentle embrace of nature's own remedies. This approach to managing pests and diseases—a confluence of ancient wisdom and modern understanding—invites gardeners to look beyond the immediate challenge and see the garden as an ecosystem where balance is key.

At the heart of natural and safe remedies is the principle of doing no harm— to the plants, the soil, the beneficial insects, and the broader environment. This ethos, deeply rooted in the tradition of organic gardening, guides the selection and application of treatments, ensuring they nourish and protect rather than degrade and harm.

Neem oil, extracted from the seeds of the neem tree, exemplifies the power and potential of natural remedies. Revered for its insecticidal and fungicidal properties, neem oil offers a broad-spectrum solution that respects the garden's balance. Applied as a foliar spray, it controls common pests like aphids and mites and battles fungal diseases without disrupting beneficial insects, those vital allies in the garden's health.

Similarly, the use of diatomaceous earth—a fine powder made from the fossilized remains of diatoms—showcases the ingenuity of natural pest control. When sprinkled around plants, its microscopic sharp edges deter slugs, beetles, and other soft-bodied pests, providing a barrier that protects without poisoning the soil or the waterways.

Companion planting, too, stands as a testament to the garden's inherent wisdom. By pairing plants that offer mutual benefits—such as marigolds, which repel nematodes and attract pollinators, or garlic, known to deter a host of pests—gardeners can fortify their gardens against pests and diseases. This strategy, woven into the garden's design, celebrates diversity and interdependence, principles that underpin a healthy, resilient garden ecosystem.

In the face of fungal diseases, the answer often lies not in the medicine cabinet but in the compost bin. Compost tea, a nutrient-rich solution brewed from decomposed organic matter, acts as both a foliar spray and a soil drench, enhancing plant health and immunity. This simple yet effective remedy illustrates the cycle of renewal at the heart of organic gardening, where waste is transformed into wealth.

The embrace of natural and safe remedies extends to the cultivation of plants themselves, selecting varieties known for their resistance to pests and diseases. This proactive approach, grounded in the understanding that prevention is the first line of defense, highlights the role of the gardener as a steward of plant genetics, choosing seeds and starts that bring resilience and vitality to the garden.

Yet, the application of natural remedies is as much an art as it is a science. It requires observation, intuition, and a willingness to learn from the garden itself. Timing is crucial, as is the recognition that less is often more. The goal is not to create a sterile environment, free from any challenge, but to maintain a dynamic balance, one that allows the garden to thrive in its complexity and diversity.

This philosophy of garden health, rooted in natural and safe remedies, is a call to gardeners to embrace a broader vision of their role. It's an invitation to participate in the garden's life, not as dominators but as collaborators, working with nature to cultivate spaces of abundance and harmony. It's a practice that enriches not just the garden but the gardener, offering lessons in patience, humility, and the interconnectedness of all life.

In the end, the choice of natural and safe remedies is more than a method of pest and disease management; it is a reflection of a deeper ethos, one that values the health of the garden and the planet. It's a commitment to a way of gardening that is sustainable, ethical, and deeply attuned to the rhythms of the natural world. This approach, woven through the fabric of the garden, creates a sanctuary that is not only productive but healing, a place where the earth's bounty is celebrated, and its balance preserved.

Chapter 8: The Harvest Cycle: From Garden to Table

Harvesting Techniques to Maximize Yield

In the cyclical journey from seed to table, the act of harvesting is not merely the culmination of months of growth and care; it is a critical phase in the garden's lifecycle, one that requires insight, precision, and a deep understanding of the rhythms of nature. To maximize yield is to engage in a dance with time, a harmonious interplay between gardener and plant, where each movement, each decision, is guided by a profound respect for the life nurtured within the soil.

Harvesting techniques that maximize yield begin with the timing. This delicate art of discernment, knowing when a fruit or vegetable has reached its peak of ripeness, its zenith of flavor and nutrition, is the gardener's first and most crucial task. It is a knowledge honed through experience, through the tactile examination of texture, the visual appraisal of color, and the olfactory assessment of fragrance. Vegetables like zucchini and cucumbers are best harvested when young and tender, before they become large and seedy. Leafy greens, on the other hand, offer a continuous bounty if harvested from the outer leaves, allowing the plant to keep producing.

The method of harvest is equally important. Gentle hands and sharp tools ensure that the removal of produce does not damage the plant or its neighbors. Techniques such as cutting rather than pulling, supporting the vine or stem with one hand while harvesting with the other, minimize stress on the plant, encouraging continued production. For root vegetables, loosening the soil around the plant before extraction can prevent damage to the root system of surrounding plants, safeguarding the garden's collective vitality.

Succession planting is another technique integral to maximizing yield. By staggering plantings of certain crops at intervals, the garden can offer a continuous harvest from early summer until frost. This approach, a strategic orchestration of the garden's timeline, ensures that as one crop is harvested, another is reaching maturity, creating a sustained flow of produce from garden to table.

Interplanting and companion planting also contribute to yield maximization. These practices, which involve growing complementary plant species in close proximity, can enhance pollination, improve the utilization of space, and even deter pests, all of which contribute to a more abundant harvest. The interplay of different plant heights, root depths, and nutrient needs creates a dynamic ecosystem where plants support each other's growth.

The health of the garden, meticulously maintained through the seasons, is the foundation upon which yield maximization rests. Soil fertility, water management, pest and disease control—all are critical components of a healthy garden, each contributing to the vigor of the plants and the abundance of the harvest. A garden tended with care, where the soil is rich, the water is sufficient, and the pests are kept at bay, is a garden that rewards the gardener with bountiful yields. Maximizing yield is also about extending the garden's productivity beyond the traditional growing season. Techniques such as the use of cold frames, greenhouses, or row covers can protect plants from early frosts, allowing for a longer growing season and, consequently, a greater harvest. Similarly, the preservation of seeds from year to year, particularly those from plants that have thrived, ensures that the garden's genetic legacy continues, adapted and resilient to its specific conditions.

The harvest itself, while the culmination of one cycle, sows the seeds for the next. The careful selection of produce for seed saving, the composting of plant residues, and the preparation of the soil for the next planting are all part of the harvest process, each step taken with an eye toward the future.

In the end, maximizing yield is not merely a series of techniques but a philosophy of gardening. It is an approach that values sustainability, respects the interconnectedness of life, and seeks harmony between the gardener and the natural world. This philosophy recognizes that the garden is a living system, a microcosm of the earth itself, and that to care for the garden is to care for the planet.

As gardeners, our role is both simple and profound: to nurture this slice of earth entrusted to our care, to learn its language, to listen to its needs, and to harvest not just the fruits of our labor but the joy and wisdom that come from living in close communion with nature. This is the essence of harvesting techniques to maximize yield, a celebration of the garden's abundance, and a testament to the gardener's art.

Storage and use of vegetables

In the garden, each vegetable harvested is a testament to the cycle of life, a symbol of the earth's generosity. Yet, the journey from garden to table does not end at harvest. The art of storing and using vegetables is a continuation of this cycle, a practice that honors the garden's abundance by ensuring that no part of the harvest goes to waste. It is here, in the careful preservation and creative use of vegetables, that the garden truly nourishes us, body and soul.

Storage, the first step in this journey, is both a science and an art. It requires an understanding of each vegetable's unique needs and the environmental conditions that will prolong its freshness. Root vegetables, for example, find solace in the cool, dark embrace of a root cellar or a storage bin filled with damp sand, mimicking the earth from which they were drawn. Here, carrots, beets, and potatoes can rest, their life extended, waiting to bring the taste of the garden to the winter table.

Leafy greens, on the other hand, crave the humidity and cold of the refrigerator. Wrapped in damp cloths or stored in perforated bags, they retain their crispness and vitality, ready to be transformed into salads, sautés, and soups. The key is moisture control—enough to prevent wilting but not so much as to invite decay.

Tomatoes, the jewels of the garden, demand special consideration. Their ripening process continues post-harvest, a slow dance of enzymes and sugars that culminates in the perfect balance of sweetness and acidity. Stored at room temperature, away from direct sunlight, they gradually reveal their full flavor, a reminder of summer days in the depth of winter.

But storage is more than just preservation; it is preparation for use. It is an anticipation of the meals to come, of the ways in which the garden's bounty will nourish family and friends. This is where creativity takes center stage, where the vegetables harvested become the inspiration for culinary exploration.

Preservation methods such as canning, freezing, and fermenting open new avenues for enjoying the harvest. Canning transforms tomatoes into sauces, salsas, and soups, capturing the essence of summer in jars that line pantry shelves. Freezing offers a way to extend the life of green beans, corn, and peas, their freshness locked in until they are ready to be enjoyed. Fermentation, an ancient practice experiencing a modern renaissance, turns cabbage into sauerkraut, cucumbers into pickles, and radishes into kimchi, adding complexity and probiotics to our diets.

Yet, the use of vegetables extends beyond preservation. It is a daily celebration of the garden's diversity. Vegetables become the stars of dishes that span the globe, from the simplicity of a roasted root vegetable medley to the complexity of a vegetable curry. They are juiced and smoothied, grilled and sautéed, eaten raw in salads, or baked into savory pies. Each dish is a discovery, an experiment, and a tribute to the garden.

The knowledge of how to store and use vegetables is passed down through generations, shared among friends, and discovered in the pages of cookbooks and gardening guides. It is knowledge that grows and evolves, reflecting changes in tastes, dietary needs, and environmental consciousness. It encourages a mindfulness about food waste, inspiring us to use every part of the vegetable, from root to leaf, in a practice of sustainable consumption that honors the resources and labor that brought it to our table.

In this way, the storage and use of vegetables become acts of gratitude, expressions of appreciation for the earth's abundance and the gardener's toil. They remind us of the connection between the food we eat and the soil it came from, a link that is often forgotten in the rush of modern life.

The garden, with its cycles of growth and rest, its rhythms of sowing and harvesting, teaches us about patience, care, and the joy of simple pleasures. The vegetables it yields, stored with care and used with creativity, are not just nourishment for the body; they are sustenance for the soul, a tangible link to the earth and to the cycles of life that sustain us.

In embracing the art of abundance—the careful storage and creative use of vegetables—we celebrate the garden's gifts and the ways in which it enriches our lives. This practice, woven into the fabric of daily life, becomes a ritual, a way of living that is deeply connected to the natural world, a testament to the beauty and bounty of the earth.

Simple recipes for enjoying your harvest

The journey from garden to table culminates in the alchemy of cooking, where the harvested bounty is transformed into dishes that nourish, delight, and celebrate the earth's generosity. This final chapter in the harvest cycle is not just about sustenance but about connection—to the food, to the land, and to each other. Simple recipes, crafted with care and respect for the ingredients, become the medium through which the garden's abundance is honored and shared. At the heart of these recipes is the garden's produce, vegetables, and fruits picked at their peak, bursting with flavor and nutrients. The beauty of garden-to-table dining lies in the simplicity of the preparation, allowing the natural tastes and textures of the ingredients to shine. A ripe tomato, a crisp cucumber, a tender zucchini—each offers a world of culinary possibilities, from the raw to the barely cooked, that celebrates their essence.

Salads are perhaps the most direct expression of the garden's bounty. Imagine a salad of mixed greens, each leaf a different shade of green, some with hints of red or purple, dressed in a vinaigrette made with herbs plucked just moments before from the garden. Add to this slices of cucumber, radish, and cherry tomatoes, each adding its crunch and burst of flavor, and you have a dish that is both a feast for the eyes and a celebration of the garden's diversity.

Soups and stews offer another avenue for garden-to-table recipes, particularly as the season transitions from summer to fall. A simple vegetable soup, started with onions and garlic softened in olive oil, can become a canvas for whatever the garden offers. Carrots, potatoes, beans, and kale, simmered together with a handful of herbs, create a dish that is both comforting and nourishing, a tangible connection to the land that sustains us.

For the abundance of zucchini that challenges even the most creative gardener, a simple sauté with garlic and a sprinkle of Parmesan can transform this prolific vegetable into a dish that is eagerly anticipated. Or consider the versatility of tomatoes, which can be enjoyed fresh in salads, cooked down into sauces, or oven-roasted with a drizzle of olive oil and herbs for a concentrated burst of flavor.

The joy of garden-to-table recipes lies not just in the eating but in the making. It's in the act of chopping and sautéing, roasting and grilling, that we engage with the produce, appreciating its beauty and imperfections, its journey from seed to table. Cooking becomes a meditative act, a time to reflect on the cycles of growth and renewal, and the labor—both ours and the earth's—that brought the food to our kitchen.

Desserts, too, have their place in the garden-to-table repertoire. Simple fruit crumbles and cobblers, where the sweetness of the fruit is enhanced by a touch of sugar and a buttery topping, celebrate the season's end. Herbs like mint and basil can add a fresh note to berries and peaches, creating dishes that are both sophisticated and unpretentious.

In sharing these meals, we share the story of the garden, of the choices and challenges, the successes and failures that marked the season. The table becomes a place of community and gratitude, where the food serves as a reminder of our connection to the earth and to each other.

Creating simple recipes to enjoy the harvest is an act of creativity and love, a way to honor the garden's abundance and the effort that brought it to fruition. It's a practice that turns every meal into a celebration, a way of living that is deeply connected to the rhythms of the natural world.

Chapter 9: Gardening Through the Seasons: Year-Round Care

Calendar of gardening tasks

Gardening, at its essence, is a dance with the seasons, a continuous cycle of growth, maintenance, and renewal that aligns with the rhythms of the earth. This dance requires not just knowledge and skill but a deep attunement to the subtle shifts in weather, light, and life that mark the passage of time. The gardener's calendar is a tool in this dance, a guide that outlines the tasks and attentions required to nurture the garden through the seasons, ensuring its health and vitality year-round.

Spring: The Awakening

As the grip of winter loosens, the garden stirs to life with the warming soil and lengthening days of spring. This season is a time of renewal and rebirth, where the gardener acts as both conductor and participant in the symphony of growth that unfolds.

The first whispers of spring call for a thorough assessment of the garden. Beds and borders are cleared of the remnants of last year's growth, making way for new life. It's a time to repair any damage that winter's harshness may have inflicted on structures and tools, ensuring everything is in readiness for the busy months ahead.

Soil preparation is paramount. Enriching the garden beds with compost and well-rotted manure revitalizes the earth, replenishing the nutrients that will fuel the season's growth. Testing the soil's pH and nutrient levels guides the gardener in making precise amendments, tailoring the soil's composition to the needs of the upcoming plantings.

Spring planting begins in earnest as the danger of frost recedes. Early vegetables like peas, lettuce, and spinach are sown directly into the prepared beds, their resilience to cool temperatures making them the perfect heralds of the garden's new cycle. Indoors, under lights and warmth, seeds of tomatoes, peppers, and other warm-weather crops germinate, beginning their journey that will eventually lead them to the sunlit garden.

Watering, though less demanding in the cool spring weather, requires vigilance. The balance of keeping the soil moist for germinating seeds and growing plants, without over-saturating, sets the stage for healthy root development. Mulching becomes a critical task, conserving moisture, regulating soil temperature, and suppressing the inevitable weeds that accompany the season's growth.

Summer: The Season of Abundance

As spring melds into summer, the garden reaches a crescendo of activity. The days lengthen, the sun strengthens, and the garden becomes a lush tableau of verdant growth and vibrant blooms.

Watering is now at the forefront of the gardener's daily tasks. The summer sun, while nurturing, can also be relentless, drawing moisture from the soil and stressing plants. The gardener's hand is steady and judicious, providing water deeply and infrequently to encourage roots to seek moisture below the surface, building resilience against the heat.

Staking and trellising become critical as plants grow tall and heavy with fruit. Tomatoes, cucumbers, and beans, among others, are supported in their upward growth, protected from the damp soil below and exposed to the sun and air that keep them healthy and productive.

Pest and disease management is vigilant during the warm months. The gardener, ever watchful, employs natural deterrents and remedies, encouraging beneficial insects and employing barriers to protect the garden's bounty. Integrated pest management strategies minimize harm to the garden's ecosystem, ensuring that control measures are as benign as possible.

Harvesting is the joy of summer. Vegetables and fruits are picked at their peak, and the garden's abundance begins to flow into the kitchen. Succession planting continues, with quick-growing crops like radishes and lettuces sown between the slower-growing vegetables, ensuring a continuous supply of fresh produce.

Autumn: The Time of Preparation

As the heat of summer wanes, the garden enters a period of transition. Autumn is a time of both harvest and preparation, a season to enjoy the fruits of the summer's labor while looking ahead to the coming winter and the next year's growth.

The harvest continues, with late-season crops like pumpkins, squashes, and root vegetables gathered. The garden is a place of bounty, and the gardener's efforts turn to preservation, storing the excess for the colder months ahead.

Preparation for winter begins. Perennials are cut back, and annuals, spent from their summer display, are removed. The soil is amended with more compost and, in some areas, cover crops are sown, protecting the earth from erosion and enriching it for the next year.

Bulbs for spring blooms are planted, a gesture of faith in the cycle of growth that will begin anew. The garden beds are mulched, protecting them from the winter chill, and tender plants are shielded with cloches or moved indoors.

Winter: The Quiet Season

With the arrival of winter, the garden rests. This season of dormancy is not idle, however; it is a time for the gardener to reflect, plan, and prepare for the year ahead. Catalogs are perused, seeds are ordered, and plans are drawn for the coming spring. It's a time for maintenance, for sharpening tools and repairing structures, ensuring that when the garden wakes, everything is in readiness for the cycle to begin again.

In each season, the gardener finds rhythm and purpose, a connection to the cycle of life that is both humbling and profound. This calendar of tasks, ever-turning, is a testament to the gardener's stewardship of the land, a dance of care and attention that sustains the garden and nourishes the soul.

Preparing for the change of seasons

The garden is a living tapestry, woven from threads of time, weather, and care. Each season paints its hues, sings its songs, and tells its tales through the soil, the plants, and the wildlife it nurtures. Preparing for the change of seasons is an art, a science, and a meditation—a practice that attunes the gardener to the subtle shifts in the environment and the needs of the garden.

As winter's chill begins to soften and the first signs of spring whisper through the thawing earth, the gardener's thoughts turn to awakening. This preparation starts with the soil, the foundation of all life in the garden. Testing the soil's nutrient levels and pH, amending it with compost and organic matter, and turning it gently to welcome the air and warmth are acts of reinvigoration, of setting the stage for the burst of life that spring will bring.

The change from spring to summer brings a crescendo of growth and activity. Preparing for this transition involves supporting the young plants as they reach for the sun—staking, trellising, and mulching to conserve moisture and suppress weeds. It's a time of vigilant pest and disease management, employing natural remedies and interventions to protect the burgeoning life. Watering strategies are refined, ensuring that each plant receives the hydration it needs to thrive in the warmth of the growing season.

As summer's abundance begins to wane and the hints of autumn's approach are felt in the cooler evenings and the golden light, the gardener's focus shifts to preservation and preparation for the coming cold. Harvesting continues, but attention also turns to saving seeds, dividing perennials, and planting bulbs that will slumber through the winter and bloom in the spring. Preparing the garden for autumn involves enriching the soil, protecting tender plants, and beginning the gradual process of putting the garden to bed.

Winter's arrival marks a time of rest for the garden, but not for the gardener. Preparing for this season of quiet involves protecting the soil with cover crops or mulch, ensuring that structures are secure against the wind and snow, and planning for the year ahead. It's a time of reflection on the successes and lessons of the past seasons, of dreaming and planning for the cycles to come. In each of these transitions, the gardener acts as both caretaker and student, learning from the garden and guiding it through the changes. This preparation is a conversation with time, a dialogue that anticipates the future while honoring the present. It requires an understanding of the garden's patterns and needs, a willingness to adapt and respond to the unexpected, and a deep respect for the forces of nature that shape our world. This engagement with the change of seasons is a celebration of the dynamic, ever-changing nature of the garden. It's an acknowledgment that the garden is not a static entity but a living, breathing organism that evolves with the cycles of the earth. Preparing for these changes is an act of partnership with the garden, a commitment to walking hand in hand with nature through the journey of the year.

The art of preparing for the change of seasons is, ultimately, a practice of mindfulness and presence. It's a way of being in the world that is attuned to the subtle shifts in the air, the soil, and the light—a way of living that is deeply connected to the rhythms of the earth. This practice enriches the gardener, not just with the tangible rewards of harvests and blooms, but with the intangible gifts of wisdom, peace, and a profound connection to the cycle of life.

In embracing the preparation for the change of seasons, we embrace the essence of gardening itself—a dance with the natural world that nurtures not just our gardens, but our souls. It's a journey of continuous learning, growth, and adaptation, a path that leads us through the beauty and challenges of each season with grace, resilience, and joy.

Renovating and restoring the garden

Renovation and restoration in the garden are acts that straddle the realms of art and science, blending creativity with ecological wisdom. They require a vision that sees beyond the immediate, recognizing the latent potential within the soil, the plants, and the garden's very layout. This vision is guided by an understanding of the garden's history, its successes and struggles, and an intimate knowledge of its character and quirks.

At the heart of garden renovation is the soil—this fundamental matrix of life that underpins all else in the garden. Restoring soil health is often the first step in the renovation process, addressing compaction, nutrient depletion, or imbalances that have accumulated over time. This restoration may involve deep digging or double-digging to aerate the soil, the addition of organic matter to improve structure and fertility, and the integration of cover crops to fix nitrogen, suppress weeds, and prevent erosion. It is a rejuvenation of the garden's foundation, ensuring it can support vibrant life for seasons to come.

Renovating a garden also frequently involves reimagining its design, adapting the layout to better meet the gardener's evolving needs and aspirations. This might mean converting underutilized spaces into productive vegetable beds, establishing new perennial borders, or creating nooks for rest and reflection. It could involve introducing water features to attract wildlife, building raised beds for easier maintenance, or incorporating paths that invite exploration and interaction with the garden's diverse zones.

The process of restoration and renovation is also deeply tied to the plants themselves, requiring decisions about which species to retain, relocate, or remove. It's a process that honors the garden's history, preserving legacy plants that contribute to its unique identity while making space for new additions that reflect current interests, environmental conditions, and design trends. This thoughtful curation of plant life is guided by principles of biodiversity, sustainability, and beauty, aiming to create a garden that is resilient, ecologically rich, and deeply satisfying to the soul.

Water management is another critical aspect of garden renovation, reflecting an awareness of the precious nature of this resource. Redesigning irrigation systems for greater efficiency, incorporating rain gardens to capture runoff, and mulching to conserve moisture are all strategies that reflect a commitment to sustainable gardening practices. These changes not only enhance the garden's resilience but also its role as a steward of the broader ecosystem.

Renovating and restoring a garden is also an opportunity to address pest and disease challenges, integrating natural barriers, companion planting, and habitat features that encourage beneficial predators. This approach to garden health is preventative, building a system that is balanced and self-regulating, reducing the need for external inputs and interventions. Throughout this process of renovation and restoration, the gardener is both architect and acolyte, shaping the garden with intention while listening to its whispers and needs. It is a dialogue, a dance of give and take that honors the garden's past, celebrates its present, and dreams of its future.

The act of renovating and restoring the garden culminates not in a final product but in a renewed relationship—a deeper bond between the gardener and the garden, forged through the shared experience of transformation. This renewed space becomes a canvas for new memories, new growth, and new discoveries, a living testament to the gardener's care, creativity, and commitment.

Conclusion

In the end, the renovated and restored garden stands as a symbol of hope and renewal, a living reflection of the cycles of life that govern the natural world. It is a space of beauty and productivity, of sanctuary and exploration, a garden that tells the story of its journey through the seasons of care and attention.

This journey of renovation and restoration is not merely a task to be completed but a way of engaging with the garden and the land that is rich in lessons and rewards. It teaches patience, humility, and the joy of seeing the garden flourish anew. It is a celebration of the gardener's art and science, an ode to the endless cycle of growth, decay, and rebirth that defines our world.

Renovating and restoring the garden is, ultimately, an act of love—a love for the garden, for the act of gardening, and for the earth itself. It is a commitment to stewardship, to sustainability, and to the belief that through our efforts, we can create spaces of beauty and abundance that nourish not just our bodies but our spirits.

Embarking on garden renovation and restoration is a profound journey that blends practical tasks with deeper philosophical engagements with the natural world. It underscores the gardener's role as a steward of the land, highlighting the continuous cycle of renewal that is at the heart of all gardening endeavors.

Chapter 10: Troubleshooting in the Garden: Solutions and Tips

Diagnosing and Solving Frequent Problems in the Garden

The process of troubleshooting in the garden necessitates a blend of scientific acumen, ecological understanding, and horticultural expertise. This sophisticated approach involves not merely the identification of symptoms but delves into the underlying causes, ensuring solutions are both effective and sustainable. As we navigate through common garden challenges, a detailed, professional methodology is paramount for achieving long-term success and vitality within our cultivated ecosystems.

Understanding plant physiology and environmental interactions is the cornerstone of advanced garden troubleshooting. For instance, chlorosis, the yellowing of leaf tissue due to insufficient chlorophyll, can be symptomatic of various stress factors including nutrient deficiencies, poor drainage, or pH imbalances. A professional approach involves conducting soil tests to accurately assess nutrient levels and pH, followed by the application of targeted amendments such as iron chelates for iron deficiency or sulfur to lower pH levels, ensuring these interventions are precisely calibrated to the plant's specific requirements.

Water management in the garden is a critical area requiring both technical knowledge and strategic planning. Over- or under-watering can lead to root diseases or physiological stress, compromising plant health. Implementing an irrigation system based on soil moisture content readings, rather than a fixed schedule, allows for responsive watering practices that align with actual plant needs. The use of drip irrigation systems and soil moisture sensors represents a technical approach to optimizing water use efficiency, reducing waste, and preventing the common pitfalls of moisture-related plant stress.

Pest and disease management within a professional framework emphasizes integrated pest management (IPM) strategies. This involves regular monitoring for pest and disease symptoms, accurate identification of the causative agents, and an understanding of their life cycles and ecological roles. Biological control measures, such as the introduction of predatory insects for aphid management, are preferred over chemical interventions for their sustainability and minimal impact on non-target species. Advanced practices also include the use of disease-resistant plant varieties and the strategic application of organic fungicides and insecticides, with a focus on timing and lifecycle stages for maximum efficacy.

Nutrient management is another domain where technical proficiency is essential. The interpretation of soil test results to diagnose nutrient imbalances requires a thorough understanding of plant nutrition and soil science. Recommendations for fertilizer application, whether organic or synthetic, should be based on specific nutrient needs, soil conditions, and crop requirements. The concept of spoon-feeding, or the application of fertilizers in small, targeted doses, minimizes leaching and environmental impact while ensuring optimal nutrient availability for plant growth.

The professional gardener must also be adept at recognizing and managing environmental and abiotic stressors that can mimic or compound biotic challenges. This includes the ability to diagnose issues related to air and soil temperature extremes, light intensity variations, and mechanical damage. Solutions may involve modifying the microclimate through the use of shade cloths, windbreaks, or mulches, as well as adjusting planting dates and locations to better suit plant species and cultivars to their growing environment. Advanced gardening troubleshooting also encompasses the use of technology and data analysis for informed decision-making. Tools such as geographic information systems (GIS) for mapping plant health and drone technology for aerial monitoring can provide valuable insights into garden conditions, allowing for precise interventions. Data-driven approaches, leveraging soil and climate data, enhance the gardener's ability to predict and mitigate potential issues before they escalate.

In essence, the transition from basic to advanced troubleshooting in the garden is marked by a shift from reactive to proactive strategies. This involves a deep dive into the intricacies of plant-environment interactions, a commitment to ongoing education and the adoption of cutting-edge technologies. By fostering a holistic and informed approach to garden management, we can ensure the health and productivity of our gardens, contributing to the sustainability of our practices and the well-being of the ecosystems we steward.

When and How to Ask for Help in the Garden

Embarking on the gardening journey, we often find ourselves standing amidst a mosaic of lush greens and vibrant blooms, feeling both awe and at times, overwhelming perplexity. The garden, with its intricate symphony of life, occasionally composes a tune that is complex for the solo gardener to decipher. It is in these moments, amidst the whispers of leaves and the hum of the earth, that the wisdom of seeking assistance becomes invaluable. The act of reaching out for help is not a testament to one's inadequacy but a bold step towards nurturing a thriving garden.

The garden is a teacher, offering lessons in patience, resilience, and the interconnectedness of nature. However, some lessons are cloaked in mystery, requiring more than a solitary gardener's knowledge to unravel. Recognizing the moment to seek guidance is akin to understanding the subtle shift in the wind's direction—it's an intuitive knowing that what lies before you demand a collaboration of minds. Whether it's the enigmatic curling of leaves, the unexplained stunting of growth, or an invasion by an unidentified pest, these are the garden's signals, urging you to extend your hand in search of knowledge beyond your garden gate.

Asking for help is an art form, blending humility with curiosity. The first step is identifying the source of wisdom that resonates with your gardening ethos. This might be a local horticultural society, where the collective wisdom of seasoned gardeners converges. Perhaps it's a master gardener program offered through cooperative extension services, providing access to a wealth of research-based knowledge. Or it could be a trusted nursery, where plants are not just sold, but are nurtured by experts who understand their language.

When reaching out, clarity in communication is the bridge that connects your query to a solution. Articulate your gardening challenge with as much detail as possible—describe what you see, what you've attempted, and even what you suspect. This narrative not only aids in diagnosing the issue but also enriches your understanding of the garden's ecosystem. Photographs can serve as powerful allies in this dialogue, capturing nuances that words might miss. Remember, every question you pose is a reflection of your commitment to the garden's wellbeing, a testament to your role as its steward.

The digital age has woven a vast web of virtual gardens, communities where the passion for planting thrives. Online forums, gardening blogs, and social media groups offer platforms where questions can be sown, awaiting the harvest of collective wisdom. Here, anonymity provides comfort to the hesitant gardener, and responses flourish like seedlings in spring. Yet, tread these paths with discernment, filtering the advice through the sieve of scientific evidence and personal intuition.

In seeking help, be open to the myriad forms in which answers may present themselves. Sometimes, the guidance you seek may not align with your expectations but consider these moments as opportunities for growth. Gardening is not merely about following a set of instructions but about engaging in a dialogue with nature, learning its rhythms, and understanding its language. The advice received, when applied, becomes a part of this ongoing conversation, a step towards deeper harmony with the living tapestry of your garden.

Moreover, asking for help is a two-way street. It is about building a community, a garden of minds where knowledge is not just taken but shared. Share your successes and failures alike, for in the tapestry of gardening, every experience adds a unique hue. By doing so, you contribute to the collective wisdom, making the journey easier or more enriched for another gardener who, someday, might find themselves standing where you once stood.

In conclusion, when and how to ask for help in the garden is a reflection of the gardener's journey towards understanding the intricate dance of nature. It is about recognizing that in the vastness of the garden's mysteries, no gardener is an island. Seeking help is an act of strength, a declaration that the health of the garden transcends individual ego. It is a step towards nurturing not just a garden of plants, but a garden of community, knowledge, and mutual growth. So, let your questions be the seeds you plant in the fertile soil of curiosity, watered by the wisdom of others, growing into a garden that flourishes beyond your wildest dreams.

Maintaining Motivation Amidst the Verdant Labyrinth

In the garden, each day dawns with the promise of growth and the potential for challenge. This verdant labyrinth, where the gardener plays both the minotaur and the hero, is a realm of endless learning and discovery. Yet, amidst this bucolic splendor, the gardener's spirit may sometimes falter, weighed down by the unyielding earth or the capricious climate.

Maintaining motivation, then, becomes not just a matter of will, but a cultivated skill, a deliberate nurturing of the soul's garden alongside that of the earth.

The essence of sustaining enthusiasm in gardening lies in the recognition of the garden as a mirror of life itself—cyclical, unpredictable, and rich with the potential for rebirth. It's understanding that every fallen leaf and every withered bloom is not an epitaph but a verse in the ongoing saga of growth. This perspective transforms setbacks into stepping stones, inviting the gardener to tread lightly over them, eyes fixed on the horizon of possibility.

Cultivating a resilient gardener's heart begins with setting realistic expectations. Just as we do not expect a seed to leap from the soil into full bloom overnight, we must temper our aspirations with patience, understanding that growth is a gradual unfolding. Celebrate the small victories—a sprout breaking ground, the first flush of flowers, the harvest of a single tomato—as fervently as you would a bountiful yield. These moments of joy, seemingly insignificant in isolation, weave together to form the tapestry of a fulfilling gardening journey.

Embracing the garden's rhythm is another key to sustaining motivation. There exists a natural ebb and flow to gardening, a seasonal symphony that plays out over the year. Align your activities with this rhythm—planning and dreaming in the winter, planting and tending in the spring, observing and nurturing in the summer, harvesting and reflecting in the fall. This cyclical approach not only ensures a balance of effort and rest but also keeps the gardener anchored to the present moment, finding contentment in the process rather than fixating solely on the outcomes.

Community plays a pivotal role in nurturing the gardener's spirit. Sharing the journey with fellow gardeners, whether through local clubs, online forums, or casual conversations over the fence, creates a web of support that can catch and uplift the gardener in moments of doubt. These connections become conduits for shared wisdom, encouragement, and inspiration, reminding us that we are not alone in our challenges. The communal exchange of stories, seeds, and saplings fosters a sense of belonging and purpose, enriching the individual experience with the collective joy of growth.

Innovation and education also serve as potent fertilizers for motivation. The garden is a classroom without walls, offering endless lessons in ecology, botany, art, and philosophy. Pursuing knowledge about new planting techniques, experimenting with different crops, or diving into the history and folklore of gardening can rekindle the spark of curiosity and drive the gardener forward with renewed purpose. Each new insight or skill acquired is a lantern lighting the path through the garden's mysteries, revealing beauty and wonder at every turn.

Finally, the practice of gratitude anchors the gardener's motivation in a profound appreciation for the garden and its gifts. To stand in the garden, inhaling the earth's perfume, feeling the soil beneath one's fingers, and witnessing the dance of light and shadow through the leaves, is to be immersed in a living, breathing work of art. Acknowledging the garden as a source of beauty, sustenance, and sanctuary fosters a deep sense of gratitude that fuels the gardener's commitment through seasons of abundance and scarcity alike.

In essence, maintaining motivation in the garden is an exercise in mindfulness, resilience, and gratitude. It is about seeing the garden not as a site of labor and toil but as a canvas of possibility, a space for growth not just of plants but of the self. By setting realistic goals, embracing the garden's rhythm, engaging with the community, pursuing continual learning, and practicing gratitude, the gardener cultivates not only a thriving garden but a resilient, joyful spirit, capable of weathering the storms and basking in the sunlight of this verdant journey.

Conclusion

As we draw the curtains on this journey through the realms of gardening, it's essential to pause and reflect on the path we've traversed together. From the initial steps of designing our green havens to the meticulous care of our plants, and through the cycles of seasons, we've embarked on a voyage that transcends the mere act of gardening. It's a pilgrimage into the heart of nature, a testament to the profound connection between earth and caretaker.

In the chapters of this book, we've explored the multifaceted aspects of gardening, from the foundational principles of soil science to the artful practices of planting and maintenance. We've delved into the challenges of pests and diseases, and celebrated the triumphant moments of harvest. Each section, meticulously crafted, was aimed not just to inform but to inspire—a guide to awaken the dormant gardener in all of us, encouraging us to reach into the soil and discover the joy of growth.

Gardening, as we've seen, is not a static endeavor confined to the boundaries of our backyards or the limits of our balconies. It's a dynamic, living process that evolves with each passing season. It's an act of creation and recreation, where each day presents a new canvas for expression and exploration. The garden is a mirror to our world, reflecting the beauty of diversity, the importance of balance, and the critical need for sustainability.

This book sought to equip you with the tools, knowledge, and confidence to embark on your gardening journey, but it also aimed to instill a deeper appreciation for the rhythms of nature. We've learned that gardening is not just about the end product—the vegetables, fruits, or flowers we cultivate. It's about the process—the moments of quiet contemplation, the lessons learned through trial and error, and the simple pleasures found in the act of nurturing life.

As we conclude, remember that gardening is a journey without a final destination. There will always be more to learn, challenges to overcome, and beauty to behold. The garden is a teacher, offering lessons in patience, resilience, and the interconnectedness of all living things. It's a sanctuary where we can find solace, inspiration, and a deeper connection to the earth.

Let this book be a starting point, a spark to ignite your passion for gardening. Take the principles, tips, and techniques shared within these pages and apply them to your unique space and circumstances. Experiment, explore, and don't be afraid to get your hands dirty. For it's through the act of gardening that we grow—not just plants, but ourselves.

In every seed planted, there's hope for a greener future, a belief in the power of growth and renewal. As you close this book and step into your garden, carry that hope with you. Nurture it, let it flourish, and share it with the world. For in the heart of every gardener lies the potential to make a difference, one plant at a time.

Thank you for joining me on this journey. May your garden be a source of joy, inspiration, and boundless discovery. Here's to the countless seasons of growth ahead, to the stories yet to be told, and to the endless possibilities that lie within the soil. Happy gardening.

Immagine di <a href="https://it.freepik.com/foto-gratuito/vista-della-rosa-che-fiorisce-in-serra_60915022.htm#page=2&query=garden&position=19&from_view=search&track=sph&uuid=b5f8b0d3-0027-41c7-81a0-78ebcc8da471">Freepik</a>

Immagine di <a href="https://it.freepik.com/foto-gratuito/piantina-di-fioritura-della-tenuta-della-mano-in-giardino_2579525.htm#page=2&query=garden&position=3&from_view=search&track=sph&uuid=b5f8b0d3-0027-41c7-81a0-78ebcc8da471">Freepik</a>

BONUS

Scan the QR Code

www.ingramcontent.com/pod-product-compliance
Lightning Source LLC
LaVergne TN
LVHW020422080526
838202LV00055B/4996